D0426224

67275   BX
                         4210
Quin   Q5

Last on the menu

Date Due

JUL 14 '70		
	WITHDRAWN	

WITHDRAWN

CHABOT
COLLEGE
LIBRARY

25555 Hesperian Boulevard
Hayward, California 94545

PRINTED IN U.S.A,

LAST ON THE MENU

LAST ON THE MENU

By

Sister Eleanor Quin
(Sister M. Vincent dePaul, C.S.J.)

PRENTICE-HALL, INC., ENGLEWOOD CLIFFS, N.J.

BX
4210
Q5

LAST ON THE MENU by Sister Eleanor Quin
© 1969 by Sister Eleanor Quin
All rights reserved. No part of this book may be
reproduced in any form or by any means, except for
the inclusion of brief quotations in a review, without
permission in writing from the publisher.
13-524033-6
Library of Congress Catalog Card Number: 78-80997
Printed in the United States of America · T
Prentice-Hall International, Inc., London
Prentice-Hall of Australia, Pty. Ltd., Sydney
Prentice-Hall of Canada, Ltd., Toronto
Prentice-Hall of India Private Ltd., New Delhi
Prentice-Hall of Japan, Inc., Tokyo

To the man in my life,
my Dad!

67275

CONTENTS

*

LAST ON THE MENU

I

The Makings

March 1951. Joanne was at the wheel of the sea-green Ford sedan, and I was wedged between her and Kathleen. Marie, Catherine, and Frances were in the back. Five of my oldest and dearest friends. They had temporarily deserted husbands and jobs to accompany me on the most important journey of my life, from upper Manhattan to Englewood Cliffs in New Jersey. Every mile of the way, directly and by innuendo, they were opening escape doors for me. In all their lives, perhaps, they had never known a less likely candidate for the convent. Nor had I. But I knew what I wanted.

Kathleen turned off the radio. "How about it?" she asked. "Ten to one you won't stay?"

"You know how I feel about gambling," I replied. She did, and so did the others. My love for one-hundred-to-one shots at Belmont was one of the reasons that I was not a wealthy woman.

"All right, have it your way," said Marie. "Twenty to one, then, and each of us will take a piece of the action. Put up your one."

I removed my earrings and my high-school class ring and handed them to Marie. "See what you can get for these," I directed. "You understand I'm a little short of cash." It was the understatement of the year. My last thirty-four dollars had been spent for the sheerest hose I'd been able to find and high-heeled navy pumps. The tailored navy suit and white blouse I was wearing had set me back considerably more. There'd been no money left for a hat, but I didn't like hats, anyway. If I do say so myself, I was quite the lady of high fashion that morning, all navy and white and red—my ample but unruly head of hair accounted for the red. The only thing wrong was the color of the Ford.

"Not that it's any of our business," said Frances, "but what did your father say when you broke the news about becoming a nun?"

"I haven't heard from him, but he's been very busy," I replied. That was both truth and assumption. He was in Florida, and he had not answered my letter. But if the horses down there weren't running on a given day, the greyhounds were at night and that meant Father was very busy, indeed. Too wise to wither away in retirement, he'd turned his hobby of studying scratch sheets into a new career.

"And as for Bill, he telephoned last night. He offered congratulations, and said he'd drink to me today."

"The Scotchman," said Joanne, and we all laughed. My only brother, four years my senior, managed a liquor store in California.

"And as for Sam?" I heard Catherine say.

"He'll recover," was about all I could say, and although I've never seen him again, it was a fine prediction. Sam did recover. Almost too quickly for my vanity. He married within two years, became a good father, and inherited the considerable family business, just as he'd promised.

His name wasn't and isn't Sam, of course, but he was real, and though he recovered, for a long time he didn't forget me completely. He sent me checks for church charities on the arrival of his first three children, all girls. His marriage has been blessed with six more arrivals since. No checks for the church. All sons, I guess.

"You could do worse than marry Sam," Catherine told me. "What's so wrong with marriage? Don't we look happy?"

"The five of you look equally happy, and two of you aren't married," I reminded her.

"Don't look at me," said Marie. "I'm never going to marry, but I don't intend to hide away in a convent, either. And you shouldn't, Ellie. You're just not the type!"

"Will all of you please stop this?" I begged. "I intend to become a nun, and that's final! Enjoy the scenery."

It had turned into a strange sort of a journey, as if they were delivering me to a torture chamber instead of St. Michael's Novitiate.

"About a mile to go," said my closest friend of all, Frances Smith. It may have been designed as a cheerful remark, but her tone of voice would have been more appropriate at a wake. Then she added, "The last mile!"

It was meant to be a humorous remark, I'm sure, but at that moment it didn't help much. Only 5,280 feet of my old life were left to me. Doubt touched me for the first time in weeks. Was I right? Who was I to be cocksure that I could be of service to man?

"I was just trying to brighten the mood," Frances explained. "We're all for you, and you must know that or we wouldn't be here. In fact, we're proud of you. Right, everybody? We're proud of you, Ellie. Of course, that doesn't mean we understand why you think you must do this and we'll miss you. But we're still proud." Then she lifted her head to help find a parking space in front of the novitiate, and, I suspect, to avoid crying.

Ten other candidates were entering that day. I was minutes early but the last to arrive—hatless, at that. The room was crowded with the parents and friends of my classmates, all there to say their good-byes.

A sister approached us, smiled as she studied each of us, and then finally beckoned to me. As I stepped forward, Marie blurted, "May we have just a few minutes with her, please?"

"You may, in a few minutes," said the sister, and she didn't speak again until we had climbed the long staircase to the third floor. "Are your eyes blue or green?"

"I don't really know," I told her. "It depends upon the light."

"Be constant in any light. They seem blue to me. This is your cell." She opened the door, and I followed her into my

4

new quarters. "There are those who say that this room in particular compares to the best at the Waldorf, but those who say it have never been to the Waldorf. Now, then, as soon as you've changed, you may rejoin your friends. I hope things fit."

Then I was alone and hurrying from my all-navy outfit into all black: maxi-skirted habit, cotton stockings, sturdy oxfords, and veil. The only relief from black was my red hair, and I wondered if it would be appropriate or necessary to dye it. The skirt was much too long and the oxfords a little small.

The sister had referred to my quarters as a cell. It was one fourth of a dormitory room that had been divided by floor-to-ceiling pale green curtains. One glance was sufficient to cover the furnishings: a plain single bed, one straight-back chair, a wooden dresser, a small hand mirror, and a prefabricated closet. Air conditioning was provided by a single window. The cell's floor space was about ten by ten. I had seen smaller rooms but hadn't lived in them.

My friends stared at me when I joined them. I half expected them to tell me I looked as beautiful as Miss America but had to be content with, "Why, Ellie, you're so dramatic in black! It's your color, it really is! To think of all the years you wasted on navy and blue! Why, if Sam could see you now . . ."

"My God, if you'll excuse the expression, we left the bag in the car!" Marie almost shouted. She fled from the parlor, unaware that the room was now quiet and all eyes were upon her.

The bag was a supermarket shopping bag, and in it were my bowling shoes and riding boots. They and the clothes I had worn to the novitiate were the only treasures from the old days that I would retain. They would remain in my trunk as a hedge against the future, just in case I became a novitiate dropout or the recipient of an invitation to leave.

Minutes later, I was standing on the outside steps, one hand clutching the shopping bag and the other waving a good-bye to my friends. As the green Ford rolled down the street and headed back to Manhattan, I was thinking that I didn't have a dime in my pockets. I had no way of knowing that one day those pockets would be bulging with millions.

And I was thinking—not as a drowning person, but as one uplifted and on the threshold of achievement—of all sorts of little things that added up to my life and were now ending.

I was baptized Eleanor Dorothy Quin. Eleanor because my mother thought it a pretty name, and Dorothy because my father had loved two women in his life and the one named Dorothy had married somebody else. Somehow, my father felt avenged. My mother didn't mind.

The baptismal took place during my third week, and the priest who officiated claimed I was the noisiest baby he'd ever had the pleasure of holding. I guess he was right, for in later years my father would often say "Eleanor Dorothy Quin, will you be quiet for a change and let a man think? You started talking when you were three weeks old and you haven't stopped since!"

Father was a thinking man, Mother was a quiet person, and brother Bill has always condensed his conversation, so my gift of gab was not inherited. Nor was the color of my hair. Genealogically speaking, I was a family freak. Indeed, if I inherited anything from the union of John and Catherine Quin, it was my father's love for horses. But did that have anything to do with genes?

John Quin was fourth-generation Manhattan. By the time I came along as his second child and only daughter, he was well established in the grocery business—that is, he owned his own neighborhood store. From the start he had three strikes against him: two chain stores on his block, buy-now-pay-later customers, and a passion for thoroughbreds which often inspired him to close his store on the busiest day of the week. Anyone looking for him on those Saturdays had to search through the throngs at Yonkers, Aqueduct, or Belmont. And sometimes, if they found him, they would also find me.

He was five-seven and thin as a rail; he never weighed more than a hundred and twenty pounds or so. He had horrified his quite proper parents by running away from home and high school to become an apprentice jockey. He'd been a good one, or so he told me, and some kind soul offered him full jockey status in France. He returned home to break the glad tidings to his parents, and they kept him there. Roosevelt Raceway was the closest he ever got to France, but he did finish high school.

John Quin started his business career as a clerk in a chain store, then switched to a delicatessen. It was the night shift, not the wages, that attracted him. The night hours left the days free for afternoons at the tracks, and there, in the long run, he made a substantial killing. It provided him with sufficient funds to marry and go into business for himself. Uncle Eddie, who was not his real uncle, loaned him some of the dollars to buy the grocery store.

I don't know where he met my mother. She was Mt. Vernon, and that didn't sit well at first with my paternal

7

grandparents, for a Quin man always married a Manhattan woman. They regarded this new Catherine in their lives as a farm girl, hardly a proper mate for a city man.

Mother was just over five feet tall and never did approve of Father's love for the nags. In all her married years she knew but one home, and that was a five-room apartment on the top floor of a five-story building. It was located on the Upper West Side of Manhattan, and that's where I was born. There was no elevator.

In the beginning the apartment had two bedrooms, a dining room, a living room, and a kitchen. Not long after my arrival the blueprint was changed, and the dining room became the third bedroom. So my brother and I had our own bedrooms, much to the envy of other children in the neighborhood. The master bedroom, or former dining room, belonged to my mother and father. It was located between the kitchen and the living room, was the scene of much traffic, and was also the reason my parents didn't entertain at home very often.

Parochial schools were close by, but Bill and I always attended public schools. My mother felt we should subject ourselves to "other points of view," whatever they were supposed to be, and my father didn't object because he considered he was getting something in return for his taxes.

I was more tomboy than pure girl. Never owned a doll and never wanted to own one. Boy games were my speed, and they ranged from cops and robbers to mini-baseball and bowling to small territorial wars. Surely the cop on the beat would have voted me the least likely of the local little girls to ever succeed in the convent.

Actually, a future in religion had not crossed my mind at that point. Instead, I saw myself as the first of the women

8

jockeys and the first lady shortstop in the history of the major leagues. But those were impractical long shots, and I knew it. Society was against them. Civilization was lagging. But I had other, more feminine dreams to fall back on: a musical-comedy star and the wife of a cowboy.

For a long time my Broadway ambition was encouraged by my father's friend Uncle Eddie, a fat, jolly man who wore the first silk suit I ever saw and had dinner with us at least once during each of his infrequent business trips to New York. His permanent address was in Reno. Now that I think about it, Uncle Eddie was quite a character. Before my bedtime he would remove a new deck of playing cards from his pocket and run the cards through a series of amazing shuffles. I think my mother died believing that he was a solid business-man, for in her presence, and I suspect for her benefit, he always cautioned my father against gambling. "Betting on horses is not a hobby, it's a disease," he would say, waving a fat forefinger in my father's face. "You can't win! Put your spare dollars into a bank. Don't you want to send your kids to college?"

Uncle Eddie could also be counted on for two orchestra seats (matinee) to a current Broadway smash—my reward for giving a small but energetic after-dinner concert of hit songs. And thanks to his little rewards, our family achieved a certain cultural status in the neighborhood. We were the only ones fortunate enough to see Broadway shows.

My mother enjoyed this status so much that it inspired her to drag her children around the city on visits to such free cultural establishments as museums, libraries, galleries, and historical sites. When the tracks weren't open, we spent many a Saturday in that way. By the time I reached my teens, I was making the trips alone, doing just what visitors to the city often do, and what city residents do—then as now—too rarely. None of the culture I absorbed helped me to master any of Uncle Eddie's shuffling techniques or become a Broadway star, but through specialization I did become something of an expert on equine history, paintings, and lore.

The Broadway dream lasted all through high school, but the other one (marrying a cowboy) was shattered when I was sweet sixteen. It was the year of my first suitor, a boy named Tommy who lived down the street and worked in the neighborhood A&P when he wasn't in school. He was tall, handsome, athletic, and owned a winning smile, all qualities I wanted in my helpmate for married life on the ranch. Truthfully, I was more his suitor than he mine, for I had to campaign to attract his attention. But it wasn't too long before Saturday night became the most important night in the week for us both. We spent some of them at the movies, others dancing our version of the lindy, and still others (the best ones) holding hands on moonlight sails around the Isle of Manhattan.

It was sweet while it lasted, but I knew it was all over the very moment he confessed that he didn't like animals and was afraid of horses. How could any woman love such a man? How could the mighty A&P employ such a man? I started to appreciate my father's resentment of chain stores.

When Saturday night came and Tommy failed to show, I was obliged to advise my parents that Tommy was no longer a part of my life. My mother was more heartbroken than I. "He's such a nice boy and he's been so good for you, if you know what I mean," was her immediate reaction to the news. I didn't know what she meant, so she explained, "Well, I mean you've been less shy and more outgoing. He's been helping to develop your personality, Ellie." There were tears in her eyes. My father almost swallowed his cigar. "Our firecracker shy?" he asked. "Tell me, Catherine, where have you been the last sixteen years?" Then he turned to me and said, "Never mind. You are 100 percent right! A man who doesn't love animals isn't worth the time of day."

He, of course, was fondest of one particular sort of animal. But I have always remembered his declaration and have found through the years that those who lack compassion for the lesser creatures are somehow incomplete human beings.

Tommy, however, wasn't the biggest bone of contention in the Quin house. My report card also caused a good deal of consternation. Many a night my mother could be heard predicting: no girl gets a C minus in conduct. She's almost a delinquent, and she doesn't seem to be improving. Please talk to her! What if she falls to D? I'll tell you what! She'll be suspended! And if a public school suspends her, what parochial school will have her?"

The C minus was not my fault, my father would always insist. The teachers were at fault, for they continued to misunderstand me. I had spirit, "the spirit of a left-hander, which science is just beginning to understand." So he never did lecture me, perhaps because his own conduct in school had not been praiseworthy, or because my brother Bill, a straight-A man in conduct, barely achieved passing grades in history, English, and Latin, subjects where I excelled. Except for conduct, I was the real student in the family, and this puzzled my mother. I never studied at home, whereas Bill plodded through a mountain of books and papers almost every night. He, of course, was right-handed, or left-brained.

My reputation as Miss Misconduct grew out of my penchant for pranks and preceded me from grade to grade—the logical consequences of which my right-brain never did seem able to grasp. At one point, Uncle Eddie tutored me in the basics of ventriloquism. Needless to say, this was a disaster—particularly since he'd neglected to teach me how to disguise the voice I was throwing.

"You were simply eager for attention and popularity, and you thought that the pranks would make you a heroine of sorts among your classmates," said the noted psychiatrist who happened to be sitting next to me at a charity dinner many years later. "If I'd known you then," he continued, "I wouldn't have said that you had the makings of a nun."

Nobody else would have, either, including myself. As Catholic families go, mine was just about average, or the kind one calls a good Catholic family: we attended Mass every Sunday. But we were not active in church affairs, and religion was rarely discussed at home.

But subtle signs to my future were there. One was in a study hall at high school. The windows faced westward to the Hudson, and on a hazy day I could always see the traffic on the George Washington Bridge. On clear days, I could see the tops of the biggest buildings in Englewood Cliffs, New Jersey. With the help of others who were familiar with that town, I was able to identify most of the buildings. One, however, remained a mystery. It had a red roof. Red tile, we thought.

And then there was the school's Newman Club. I joined it because my mother insisted that I join some sort of a club, it met at a convenient hour, the faculty leader was the handsomest male I'd ever seen, and my history teacher thought it would broaden my knowledge of God and the world. It did.

Many of the late (1890) John Henry Newman's theories were over my head, but for the first time I started thinking seriously about religion, although never dreaming where it would lead.

I did become a high-school graduate, and I was voted "the only freckled redhead likely to succeed." It wasn't much of an honor. I was the only freckled redhead in the class.

College was out. Those "crooked track people" continued to ruin my father's wise investments, and the Quin family never did boast much of a savings account. Uncle Eddie, who might have helped, hadn't been around in a couple of years.

So I had to find a job.

I found it hard to believe that the future of America was in my hands, yet that's what the commencement speaker had told me (and a few hundred others) on graduation day. Until then, I had assumed that the future was in the hands of Franklin Delano Roosevelt, Fiorello H. La Guardia, Maxwell Anderson, Marie Dressler, John L. Lewis, and Mickey and Minnie Mouse. The national economy was struggling out of the depths of the Depression, but all of them were going fine. I was perfectly willing to leave the future in their hands.

For a period of weeks it looked as if I would have to do that, for my job credentials didn't amount to much: (1) nonsalaried assistant at a riding stable, (2) nonsalaried clerk in my father's store, and (3) part-time clerk at department stores during holiday seasons. I had been on salary in the latter category, of course, but had always fallen victim to department-store strategy or special discounts for employees. I planned the spending of each paycheck down to the last penny, and the money went for the latest authentic copies of the hottest Paris fashions. For everything but hats.

The search for employment was rather lackadaisical. I was willing to spend another carefree summer in the Adirondacks before settling down into the role of wage earner. I had stars in my eyes and knew that the coming fall could be the promising season for me. Hadn't *Variety* predicted that show biz, with over a dozen musicals promised, would be in a desperate hunt for new faces? Didn't I have dramatic talent, a beautiful voice, flaming red hair, and a letter of recommendation from my high-school dramatic director–biology teacher? How could I miss? All I had to do was wait for casting to begin.

The wonderful bubble burst in late June. "We're not going to the mountains this summer," my mother announced. "Your father and I have decided to save every dollar that we can and send you to college next year. A girl with your high marks deserves a college education." She didn't mention my past conduct. "Bill says he'll help as much as he can, and you'll be expected to save as much as you can from your future wages.

I didn't think it fair for the others to sacrifice their pleasures for me, and I told her so. But she considered the situation to be a blessing: her husband and my father had sworn off going to the tracks. She would have been unhappy if she'd known what I knew: the owner of the barbershop next door to the Quin grocery store was a bookie.

Now I started hunting in earnest for a job, and in early July the rumor swept the neighborhood that talented Ellie Quin had won a place on Broadway. The rumor was a fact, of a sort. My role was that of a sales clerk in a retail store right in the heart of the theater district. In reality, it was more tourist trap than anything else, and it did a thriving business in silk neckties, although I doubt that any of the material had ever known a silk worm.

The hours were long. The store was open from ten in the morning until about midnight, when all tourists were presumed to be safely in bed, and Broadway's strange assortment of night people, few of whom wore ties, were out in force. The boss manned the cash register near the door, while his wife and I did the selling. During slack periods, we rearranged the stacks of neckties.

Each day started with the same instructions from the boss. "Don't forget to watch customers who can't make up their minds. They're probably thieves." Another one was, "If anyone wonders why we can offer this deluxe merchandise at such low prices, just say we have special contacts in the Far East, where labor is cheap." He considered Brooklyn to be the Far East.

My starting salary for the six-day week was twenty-two dollars. This was supposed to increase as I acquired sales skill, and by August I was sure my skill had improved, and I asked for a raise. To my surprise, business had not been up to expectations, although it seemed to me that I had personally sold some fifty million ties. My salary declined to twenty a week, but I kept this news from my parents. They hadn't thought much of the job from the beginning, but to me it was better than nothing at all, and it was in a favorable location. It was only logical to assume that one fine day a Broadway producer or casting director might need a necktie in a hurry, rush into the store, and discover talented little me. If it could happen to Lana Turner in a drugstore, then it could happen to Eleanor Quin in a necktie emporium.

But it didn't. The pleasant, hopeless dream exploded into nothingness on the second Monday in September. The store was empty, the door was locked, and there was a For Rent sign in the window.

So that was my first job, and while it was not a meaningful period of my life, it is the reason for startled expressions on the faces of people who ask me if I planned on becoming a nun while I was a schoolgirl. "No, and as a matter of fact, my first job was on Broadway," I reply, and they never press me for details.

"Meaningful" is an overused word these days, but it is appropriate for my second step up the ladder as a Manhattan career woman. I became a nurse's aide at a local hospital, and learned, perhaps for the first time, that the rich can be touched by misery, too.

In those days, if one really had to go to a hospital, this was the place to go. Its high rates and excellent services gave it a sort of social status, and on any given day its roster of private-room patients contained a sprinkling of film stars, leaders of industry, society figures, sports stars, government officials, and other famous names. A patient didn't have to be wealthy, but it helped.

As a nurse's aide, one didn't have to know anything about nursing, so I was more than qualified. I was assigned to what the nurses called Difficult Alley, which consisted of those particular private rooms boasting patients who were not making life any easier for the hospital staff. My assignment was simple: "Keep them happy."

My smile became as fixed as a chorus girl's as I made the

rounds on that first day, trying to bring sunshine into the lives of people who, for the most part, seemed to resent the sun. None were critical cases, all were convalescent, and they seemed to think that the hospital was very poorly run. I had thought the job would be a lead-pipe cinch, but at day's end I thought that I had earned every penny of my thirty-five dollars per week.

"Did you try to talk to them?" my father asked that night.

"I talked until I was blue in the face," I confessed.

"That's the trouble, Ellie. You have the Irish gift of gab, and you've developed it into a fine art. Now listen to me. Any fool can talk day and night, but it takes real ability to listen. Just give those poor sick people a chance to talk."

"They don't want to talk."

"They will if you provide the opportunity. Ask questions."

It was sound advice, and also the reason that I switched from reading the morning tabloids and their comics to *The New York Times*. Clark Gable was not among my patients, but if he had been, I would have questioned him about the sudden drop in General Motors stock. For twenty minutes, the grumpiest man in the hospital talked on and on about the unknown (to me) world of stocks and bonds. I didn't escape until his nurse arrived to take his blood pressure, and his parting words to me were "Hold on to General Motors."

I was not one to keep a diary, and the only written memento of my career as a nurse's aide consisted of three typewritten pages which I hunted-and-pecked at the behest of my mother. Perhaps because she felt that my ten months at the hospital should not have been in vain, she asked me toward the end of my days there to write down the most important things I had learned. There's no Quin around these days who knows where those three pages are, but I last saw them ten years or so ago and can now recall some of the new education I achieved as a nurse's aide:

Trouble is not the exclusive property of the poor.

Women are better able to cope with hardship.

Interest pays dividends. And by that I mean interest in others broadens one's views and understanding of life in this world. It couldn't have been an original thought and might have been inspired by the ailing elderly millionairess who was devoting all of her time and most of her money to various charities for the underpriviliged.

I wrote down other lessons learned, but those I've mentioned were the important ones. A lesson that I neglected to place on the report was one about a major difference between the sexes. On the wealthy level, at least, the ailing ladies were more optimistic about their futures, while the men were more suspicious of their doctors. Belief, or a willingness to believe, ran stronger in the gentler sex. I hadn't noticed that quality before.

I learned how to listen, of course, but that didn't stop me from doing my share of talking in or out of the hospital. I was the envy of many a young lady for blocks around my West Side home, for I wasn't at all shy about broadcasting the news that the likes of Katharine Hepburn, Madame Chiang Kai-shek, Spencer Tracy, and the Windsors were at the Hospital. From the tone of my voice everyone sensed that I was on a first-name basis with all of them. In all truth, the big names were not always on Difficult Alley. Indeed, Madame Chiang had a whole floor to herself and came completely staffed with Orientals. I was turned back when I tried to visit her one day. The Windsors, on the other hand, did not have a floor or even a personal staff. Just a couple of pugs. I never met either the royal couple or their pet dogs.

The temptation to study nursing was strong, but not as strong as my mother's insistence that every girl needed a college education before deciding upon a career. "Times have changed," she insisted, "and these days you can't go very far without a college education. Besides, you'll want to marry, and a college man doesn't look twice at a girl with only a high-school diploma."

So I put the hospital and thoughts of nursing behind me and entered Fordham University, all costs underwritten by the Quin family's savings. I was launched on a college career that would prove limited, but I enjoyed every minute of it while it lasted, especially the social side. Any doubts that I wouldn't be able to readjust to the academic life vanished in the first few weeks. Learning still came naturally, and I was able to take all courses in stride. If I was getting ahead in the world, it was entirely without a great deal of mental effort. In short, I was an average co-ed, dedicated to the proposition that classes are time spans wherein one makes contacts that lead to higher forms of education: dinners, dances, theaters, and sporting events.

And yet, signs pointing to my future were beginning to appear, although like the Newman Club in high school, I didn't recognize them. Among my new friends were several who attended daily Mass. I joined them, but more out of a sense of guilt than anything else, perhaps, for I was aware that my parents had made many sacrifices to send me to college, and I wasn't living up to their expectations.

Through those same friends I was introduced to the world of retreat. Again, retreats were not on the Fordham curriculum, but by the judicious cutting of classes I was able to make a three-day retreat in a Manhattan convent. It was a time for introspection—something new in my life and indispensable in every life—and for a deeper appreciation of God and the world we live in. If anyone had ever asked me the most important lesson learned at Fordham, I would have unhesitantly replied, "Retreat."

I never did become a sophomore. My mother's health had been failing for a long time, but she was the sort of woman who believed that doctors were for everybody else. The month of June sent her into a sudden decline, and for weeks her life was in the balance. She would recover and live another ten years, but never again in full health, with long relapses when she would be confined to her bed. The former nurse's aide returned home to serve as nurse, cook, and general housekeeper.

My sole contact with Fordham after that was Sam. I had dated other undergraduates, but he proved to be the one who didn't forget me. My father's pet name for him was Old Faithful, and my mother's was Mr. Saturday Night. Those names tell the story of a long enduring friendship (for me) and a patient romance (for him). From the very start, I knew we could never be more than good friends. I'm not sure just what sort of Prince Charming I was looking for in those days, but Sam required a mother more than a wife, or better yet, a combination of the two. This was one role I did not feel I could play, despite my experience on Broadway.

Not that I had ruled out marriage. Then, as now, I considered it a worthy institution for responsible people, but somehow felt that one could live a full life without it. Today I'm one of a million nuns who hold to that thesis, and all of us find it unfortunately ironic at times that we spend so much of our time and energy on children from broken homes. Boredom, the giant killer of marriages, is not a part of our lives. We don't miss it or the many forms it takes (depression, bridge and cocktail parties, adultery, etc.), nor do we miss the proven rewards of matrimony. How can one miss something one has never known?

At that stage, too, I had no definite ideas about what I wanted to do in life. Those adolescent daydreams had all been replaced by a hazy determination to make a name for myself in the world of big business, and a dozen different careers appealed to me. All I lacked were the qualifications and freedom from home responsibilities.

Finally, and happily, Mother's health had improved to the point where she insisted on managing the house by herself. By then, however, the Quin family was in poor financial shape and my father—the great champion of the small businessman —made the supreme sacrifice: he closed his store and joined forces with the hated enemy as a branch manager for the A&P. The money was better, but it wasn't enough. So to help meet our obligations (most of them medical), I returned to work.

Over the next several years I managed to find and hold a dozen different jobs in the secretarial field. My ability to type —learned while I was in Fordham but not at Fordham—came in handy. The average term of employment was about six months, a record that eventually made me look like a job hopper, but that wasn't the case. At least once and sometimes twice during a year, my mother would suffer a relapse and I would return home to manage the nursing and domestic chores.

The last of the short-term jobs was with a travel agency. I started it with high expectations, for it was my understanding that travel agents saw the world at discount rates and often with all expenses paid, as in the case of a new resort hotel opening in Bombay. Unfortunately, this understanding was true for travel agents, but false for travel-agent secretaries. Still, it was a pleasant, pressureless job, and there was always time to chat with clients who loved to talk about places they had already visited. And I made an interesting discovery: schoolteachers seemed to travel more than the members of any other profession. I hadn't thought about teaching as a career, but now I started giving it some serious attention.

My mother thought it was a splendid idea. Sam objected on the grounds that he was doing very well in his father's business and didn't need a working wife. My father wasn't sure: "There's such a thing as too much education. The thing we all want is happiness, but the highly educated people I know all seem to be unhappy. Maybe it's better to be stupid, or too dumb to know that you're unhappy."

The moment of decision about teaching never arrived because of an unforeseen event. One of the stars of Difficult Alley at the hospital arrived at our agency to discuss travel arrangements for her trip abroad.

The day she was due, even the boss was excited. Adding her to his list of satisfied clients was bound to attract more business from her circle of friends. To the disappointment of the sales staff, he planned to handle all discussions with her in person, an honor reserved for diplomats, movie stars, and the

Mafia. All of us were warned not to intrude. From the moment the great lady arrived until the time she departed, she would be the private property of the big boss.

The warning was delivered to all present at a little before noon, and it complicated my plan of at least exchanging a greeting with her. My desk was far removed from the private office of the boss, but I solved my problem at twelve ten by planting myself at an empty desk just outside his office door. At that moment the boss was hovering near the agency's front door.

Sure enough and just as promised, the lady arrived at twelve fifteen sharp. I smiled at her as the boss escorted her past my desk and into his office, but I didn't catch her eye. So I just sat there, hopeful that she might see me when the big conference was over.

Then the unexpected happened. The boss popped out of his office and beckoned to me. He was all smiles as he took my arm and brought me to the elderly lady.

"Yes, you are the same Miss Quin," she said. "Don't you recognize me? I was your patient at that silly hospital."

We chatted for a few minutes and laughed about the old days at the hospital as if we were a couple of veterans who had been through the same war. Then to my surprise and the boss's embarrassment, she asked about my salary at the agency. I think it was fifty dollars a week. The look she sent toward the boss inspired him to announce that while I hadn't been with him long, I had certainly proven myself and was due for a promotion in the near future. He was very happy when I accepted her kind invitation to lunch and returned to my own desk. To this day, I don't know whether she became a client of his or not.

I was accustomed to riding in hired limousines, mostly to funerals, but riding in a private limousine was a brand-new experience. We rode up Lexington Avenue, then over to Park Avenue, and then down Park to the Colony Club. It was (and remains today) a private club for ladies of proper lineage, social standing, and wherewithal. So proper that gentlemen were not allowed inside the doors, as if in defiance of the Harvard Club, where ladies were stopped at the door. Since then, of course, the rules have changed at both clubs, and Manhattan has somehow been able to survive the social shock.

After a wonderful lunch and a pleasant two hours, we proceeded by private limousine again to the headquarters of a national airline. There we dropped in for a friendly chat with her favorite nephew, who was one of several-score vice-presidents. He was one of the brightest men I have ever met. It didn't take him long to grasp the true reason for our visit. The combination of my charm and his future inheritance worked wonders. If I recall his words correctly, I had been born to work only in his airline's personnel department. I reported for duty the following Monday at an even hundred dollars a week.

The Quins washed down dinner with champagne that night.

I never returned to the travel agency. It's still there in mid-Manhattan, and I often pass by its doors. My old employer is gone, and now his children run the business, and it still owes me for one and a half days of labor. Sometimes I'm tempted to drop in, and perhaps I will one of these days. When a nun claims she's been cheated out of fifteen dollars and change, and claims both that sum and the accrued interest of the years, the expressions on the faces of the top brass should be something to see!

And since that great day in her nephew's office, I've never seen my chief benefactress again. She died a long time ago. I was the least of her charities, but I remain as indebted to her as do all the worthy ones remembered in her will. People like her come along now and then, but there are never enough for this troubled world.

Sometimes it's useless to deny a rumor, especially one that has been around for years and has somehow become accepted as a fact. Nonetheless, I stay right in there trying to set the record straight. Press notices and formal introductions to the contrary, I was never an airline hostess. I may have been one of the first of the flying nuns, but I was never an airline hostess!

This glamorous, false reputation probably started with my own father. Boasting was a part of his true Irish nature, and ever since he'd retired from the tracks, he'd had very little material worthy of boasting. So, soon after I started working for the airline, he was happy to inform his friends, associates, customers, and anyone else who would listen that his daughter, Ellie, formerly of Broadway, had become an airline hostess. My mother corrected him and I corrected him, but he saw no wrong in his paternal version of my career. "It's a matter of association, really. The airline employs some women as clerks and some as hostesses. Who wants to hear about a clerk? Besides, I always mention the name of the airline. Free advertising, in a way. Do you think I should be paid?"

I was with the airline for five years and eventually did give

67275

my father something to brag about. I became the only New York "clerk" to visit the airline's other offices throughout the United States. So what I hadn't found at the travel agency became a reality with the airline: plenty of free travel; better still, being paid to travel. That's the way I saw the United States. As it turned out, I was away from home more than I was at home. And by then home wasn't the one I'd known for most of my life. It was a single room in a hotel for women. My mother had died, my father had drifted to Florida, and my brother was a married man and settled in California. Uncle Eddie was gone, too. I had discovered that on my first business trip to Reno I was told that he was a genius at dealing and had no peer in blackjack.

The man my father called Old Faithful, my good friend Sam, was my only real tie to the old days. He objected to my frequent absences, and to appease him as much as to satisfy my own inquiring mind, I started looking around for a more intellectually demanding job.

I found it by accident on a mountain slope in Vermont. Or, to be precise, just after an accident. After two years of skiing, I was just coming out of my first artistic Christie when a friendly tree rushed from the forest to greet me. We met, and the first person to reach me and discover that I was still alive was a gentleman I had chatted with many times on flights to Chicago and California. He was an executive in the advertising world.

I dined with the gentleman, his wife, and two daughters that night, and drove back with them to Manhattan two days later. By then, I had been persuaded to join the Madison Avenue set as a copywriter for an advertising agency. For the first

26

time in my life, my annual income would be in five figures. The starting salary stunned the "clerks" I left behind. They dubbed me Wealthy Ellie, Girl Attaché Case.

As the months slipped by, my new wealth was not reflected by my bank account. I believed in thrift, but not to the detriment of fashion, and on Madison Avenue one had to dress several months in advance of *Vogue*. Indeed, the garments one wore seemed just as important as one's talent. Lacking the latter, a career woman could still advance if she looked like a success story. It sounds wild, but that's the way it was *circa* 1950, and maybe that's the way it is today.

I wasn't worried about my personal finances and wasn't saving for a rainy day. For a rainy day I had a chic British import. It proved not to be waterproof, but it was too smart to discard. In addition, I had two people worrying for me, my dear friend Frances Smith and her mother. Between them, they hatched a savings-fund scheme for me. This was finally activated toward the end of my first year as a big spender. Every payday, I handed over a set, small sum to Frances. In turn, she delivered this to her mother. In her turn, Mrs. Smith placed it in a savings account that was in her name. I was not told the name of the bank. I don't know why.

It was clearly understood that I could not regain one penny of my hard-earned money unless I could prove dire need. The sole judge of the legitimacy of my plea would be Mrs. Smith, and there would be no court of appeal. To her, a bridal gown represented dire need.

I met my obligation most weeks, and at the end of two years the special account was close to four hundred dollars. That was my estimate. Mrs. Smith would not divulge the exact amount. She suspected that I wanted to spend all of it, which was precisely what I had in mind. And I wasn't about to tell her what I had in mind, for I wasn't quite sure.

I was only sure that the advertising world was not for me. Still, and although it doesn't seem to have changed at all since we parted company, I'm grateful to it. In a strange sort of way, it taught me that I'd spent too many years going nowhere and that it was high time I found the road I wanted to walk for the rest of my life.

Aside from the money, I found no satisfaction in the land of coined words, ulcers, tensions, and something remembered as "anything goes" (so long as it moves the product). Oh, it had its code of ethics, but the code was something to be remembered and forgotten at convention time, and to be interpreted by individual agencies as they saw fit. And there were certain restraining powers, such as *The New York Times*. It hated superlatives, and on days when an ad proclaiming something as "The world's finest" appeared in its pages, somebody on *The Times* was asleep. My, how *The Times* has changed!

The average ad we turned out wasn't exactly misleading, but it wasn't non-misleading either. At my agency the word "good" was considered misleading, for anything represented by us had to be gooder-than-good, even if it was no good at all. On the day I turned in some copy that read, "So good a soap that it doesn't float," I was almost sent into exile. "Only morons buy good things," I was informed by my copy chief, who had missed the whole point of the slogan. I thought he was kidding and reminded him that "Good to the last drop" was one of the most successful slogans in advertising history. "It's still lousy," he told me. "Change that first word to delicious and sales would triple." I toyed with the idea of writing about a delicious soap, but refrained.

The brilliant young ladies at the agency regarded the copy chief as a pretty fair (good?) catch. But he was between wives three and four and thus a rather wary man, and dated no one at the office. It took him several years to break this golden rule, and he did it by inviting me to dinner and a movie. I accepted, of course. Along Madison Avenue, one did not refuse a date with one's boss, even if he had three wives at the time.

"I hear it's a good movie," he said during dinner. I smiled. He had uttered the forbidden word. "I didn't hear it at the agency," he explained.

As we taxied to the Normandie Theatre, he remarked that I'd seemed unhappy of late. "More ashamed than unhappy," I admitted. "Advertising is a sham, and I'm a part of it. A very tiny part, I'll admit, but what a way to earn a living!"

"Every competitive business is part true and part false," he insisted. "The nice thing about ours is that we're right out there in the open, and it's up to the intelligent consumer to decide whether we're lying or not. So we're not immoral, and we certainly aren't robbing any banks. Besides, where else can you make such an easy dollar? By convincing people to buy things they don't necessarily need or want, we're helping industry, making this country greater, and—in a cockeyed sort of way—serving mankind."

The movie we saw at the Normandie that night impressed me far more than him. Indeed, I returned on the following Saturday and Sunday and sat through it three more times. It was the French-produced film *Monsieur Vincent*, starring Pierre Fresnay as St. Vincent de Paul (1576-1660). This priest was about three centuries ahead of the Ecumenical Council and was truly dedicated to every man. Nothing dimmed his spirit, not even the Barbary pirates who sold him into slavery. He was the first to tell the Sisters of France to make the gutter their cloister so that they might find, know, and help the poor. It sounds much more advanced and philosophical in French.

I couldn't forget that film of a man who could have been an outstanding success at almost anything and yet devoted himself to the service of everyman. And it seemed almost symbolic to me that actor Fresnay rejected the role twice, and then having recovered from a near fatal accident, reread the manuscript again and accepted the role, and gave every franc of his wages to his church. (I'm often asked, "How did you happen to become a nun?" and sometimes I reply: "One night a thrice-divorced man took me to see an old French movie." That always gives the questioner something to think about.)

Within the month I made a three-day retreat and took a long, hard look at myself. Mr. Right hadn't come along, and I wasn't sure that he ever would. But even if he did, would it be right to devote the rest of my life to one man, or to helping all who needed help?

I visited my priest and told him, "I have an idea that the convent is for me, but I am not in love with the idea. What do you think?"

He lit his pipe and took a long time before answering with, "How long have I known you? Fifteen years? Well, I think I am the most surprised priest in this world."

Father Murphy was an outspoken individual. "To use one

of your advertising maxims," he said, "you've got to believe in your product."

I didn't correct him. It was a gimmick, not a maxim, and it was invented to please clients.

"In other words, no ifs, ands, and buts," he continued. "It's all the way, or forget about it, but to my mind it's not a difficult decision to make. I had to make it myself, you know. God didn't send me an engraved invitation, and don't you wait for one, either. When I reached the last bridge, I almost turned back, for I was feeling rather sorry for myself. Was I sacrificing too much? The pleasures of a woman, the joys of my own family?"

"You thought them unimportant?"

"Not at all! They were very important. Plus signs for staying where I was. And then I added up all the plus signs and all the minus signs on both sides of the bridge. The minuses were about equal. As I recall, there were seventeen pluses on the other side, as opposed to fourteen in hand. So I crossed the bridge. You can understand that I was rational about it, and not at all hasty."

We met several more times during the ensuing weeks. He insisted that the decision would be mine alone to make, and that he would not influence me one way or the other. But he did, perhaps unknowingly, on the day he drew a portrait of my personality.

"I'll tell you something about yourself," he began. "Like it or not, life has molded you into a strong, aggressive, dominating sort of woman. I can tell you that few men like to be dominated night and day. And if by some rare chance you married a man who didn't mind, you wouldn't tolerate him for long. So your only chance of a happy marriage is with a strong and dominating husband. A risky chance, too, for sooner or later one of you would bash the other over the head, and all of your offspring would be warriors at birth."

Father Murphy's appraisal, frank if not flattering, was the final push I needed. My mind was made up when I left him that day, and within the week I had started down the road that would lead me first to the novitiate and then to the convent.

Sam was the first to know. I told him on New Year's Eve an annual date with us, for he always liked to renew his proposal as early in the new year as possible. This time I told him that two dominating people could never hope for a successful marriage. The two people I had in mind were myself, for I would surely have to lead him, and his mother, who would certainly try to lead me. But Sam, of course, thought I was referring to him. The discovery that he owned a dominating personality gave Sam enormous pleasure and helped soften the blow of yet another turndown. When we parted in the early hours, we were just good friends, and I had promised to have my last date with him, and he had promised not to propose on that date. The Rainbow Room, a carriage ride through Central Park, the Village Barn, and the view from the Empire State, were all on the itinerary.

Next, I broke the news to Frances and her mother. "We knew you had something on your mind," said Mrs. Smith, "but we thought it would be something wild, such as deep-sea diving for sunken treasures."

So they were surprised, but enthusiastic, and both insisted on becoming my immediate family and accompanying me on my first visit to St. Michael's Novitiate in Englewood Cliffs. I'd been provisionally accepted for entry as a postulant in March, and I suppose everyone there wanted a look at me as much as I wanted a look at them. While I didn't anticipate difficulty, a poor impression on my part might cause them to change their minds about me. As proof of my own sincerity, I intended to bring along the sum of two hundred and fifty dollars.

This money was not required of postulants, but it was suggested as a hedge against a possible rainy day which could occur for any of many reasons: failure to make the grade, a personal decision not to continue, or a change of heart on both sides, as examples. On the day the candidate departed from the novitiate, the sum would be returned to her, along with the clothes she had worn upon entering, as well as any small personal belongings she might have saved (books, family photographs, personal papers, etc.). So, if the necessity arose, the departing one would have a stake for a fresh start in the world. Is it possible that the penal system borrowed this idea from the Church?

On a sleety day in late January, the Smiths met me on a West Side corner. There we boarded a bus that would take us across the George Washington Bridge and on to Englewood Cliffs, and to within three blocks of St. Michael's. On the way, Mrs. Smith delivered into my hands the paper money and coins that added up to three hundred and seventy-eight dollars and nineteen cents. It was the sum from my own earnings (plus interest) that she had saved for me in the secret bank. I had every intention of blowing the excess over two hundred and fifty dollars on a fashionable outfit that I would wear only twice: on the final date with Sam and to the novitiate in March.

The total sum was less than I'd anticipated. After all, I had been thrifty for almost two years. But not every week.

I was wearing a shoulder bag that day and placed the money in it. And then we talked of nonfiscal matters all the way to Englewood Cliffs.

I was the last of about twenty people to get off the bus, but the only one to slip and fall as I stepped to the sidewalk. Two gallant gentlemen lifted me to my feet and then hurried off. My face told them that I was ready to weep. The fall had ended in sort of a bellyslide over the wet and mushy concrete, and the front of my very best high-fashion coat was a mess! Frances ran into a corner coffee shop and returned with paper towels. The scrubbing wasn't of much help. Nor was my left ankle. Twisting it had been the reason for my fall, and now I was limping.

I had a Smith on my left and one on my right, both helping me as we walked to the novitiate. On that day when impressions were so very important, I looked more like a war casualty than a potential postulant.

Bill Miller's Riviera loomed up ahead. We turned a corner, marched past a huge restaurant, and came to St. Michael's. I stopped and said to my friends, "Just a minute. Before we go in, I want to tell you a little story." Seeing the Riviera had reminded me of something.

My companions came to a halt, but before I had a chance to say more, Frances shouted, "Where's your shoulder bag?"

It was certainly not attached to one of my shoulders. I had left it, and all the money in it, on my seat in the bus! My minor accident while stepping off the bus had caused all of us to for-get about the bag.

Frances ran back to the bus stop, but the bus had long since departed. And so had all thoughts of the story I wanted to tell the Smith's: of those long-ago days in high school when I'd spent hours gazing out of the study-hall window and had never been able to identify the building with the red tile roof in Englewood Cliffs. The mysterious building was St. Mi-chael's Novitiate, of course. Coincidence? I don't think so. I told that story to the Smiths on another day.

On this day in January we discovered that I wasn't the only hopeful postulant visiting St. Michael's. There were five or six others, all with their parents, but I was the only limping candidate, and the only one who looked as if she had chosen a route through a swamp. I felt like an idiot, but I wanted everybody to know that I was an honest idiot with honorable intentions, so I explained about my money that was riding the bus.

Sister Roberta smiled and asked, "Have you prayed for the return of the money?"

I confessed that I hadn't.

"Come with me," she directed. I followed her into an office. She pointed to a telephone book, then to a telephone. "I hope you can remember the name of the bus company. Call the company first, and then pray, and don't forget to put in a word of thanks for inventor Don Ameche."

I phoned the bus company. The lady in Lost and Found tried to be helpful, but I didn't know the bus's number or the driver's name or the precise time of our arrival in Englewood Cliffs.

"We'll check it through," she promised. "Perhaps we'll find the bag, but forget about the money. You know how passengers are."

"The driver looks a bit like my brother Bill, if that helps," I told her.

"It doesn't. Where can we reach you? Just in case you're lucky."

I prayed before returning to my friends and Sister Roberta, but can't recall mentioning Mr. Ameche. We remained in the novitiate for over an hour, and then proceeded back to the bus stop for the return trip to Manhattan. By then the sleet had turned to driving rain, and it seemed wisest to wait for our bus inside the corner coffee shop. There, over hot coffees, we discussed the results of our visit to St. Michael's.

"I think I blew my chances," I told the Smiths.

"Anyone can slip and fall," said Mrs. Smith. "Of course, one of us should have phoned the bus company while the other two prayed. Even before we went in, I mean. So we're all to blame."

So she didn't help my mood, nor did her daughter, Frances, with, "Next time you try for a novitiate, bring two other people along. I guess we're bad-luck charms."

As we left the coffee shop, Mrs. Smith offered the only ray of sunshine: "While I don't understand how you can be so careless about money, it does prove that you think little of worldly things, so that might help some."

We timed our coffee break perfectly. Two busses were rolling down the avenue in our direction. The first one stopped for us, and as Frances started to help me aboard, I stopped and yelled "Bill, Bill, Bill" at the driver of the second bus.

The bus was empty and passing ours, and the driver looked familiar. "It's the bus we were on before!" I explained to Frances.

She galloped off, yelling at the top of her voice. The empty bus pulled over to the curb. The driver had heard one of us! I limped as fast as I could for that second bus!

"Your friend here tells me that you lost your shoulder bag," said the driver. "A red one?"

"A blue one!"

"Well, this is your lucky day," he said, and he gave me my bag. "I found it at the end of my run. I must have had the first load of honest customers in bus history. No identification in it, but then I remembered you. You were my first redhead of the day. I'm partial to redheads. But how did you know my name was Bill? No thanks."

I was trying to give him ten dollars. "This morning, when you picked us up in Manhattan, I thought that you resembled my brother. Please take this. You don't know what this means to me."

He wouldn't accept a penny, so I said, "I'll tell you a secret. For the rest of your life, you'll never have to worry about anything. I'm going to become a nun, and I'll pray for you every day."

He grinned and said, "In that case, I'll tell you a secret. Let's not waste those prayers. My name isn't Bill. My name is Elijah, or Eli for short."

Elijah Rosenbloom was headed back for the garage. The other bus hadn't waited for us, and another wasn't due for an hour. That gave us ample time to return to the novitiate, and there I deposited my two hundred and fifty dollars.

I told the whole story of just how the money had been recovered to Sister Roberta. "A sort of miracle, wouldn't you say?" I asked.

"Not at all," she replied. "These things happen to us all the time. It's a matter of simple faith."

I gave the advertising agency a month's notice.

"Found a better job?" asked the copy chief who had taken me to the Normandie.

"A better life," I said. "I'm going to be a Sister."

He stared at me before replying, "Well, I guess you aren't kidding. But I did know something was in the wind because your copy has been consistently dreadful of late. Simple, and direct. That's no way. Detergents need romance."

A few days later he informed me that *Advertising Age* wanted to interview me. "The editor says you're making Madison Avenue history. The first ad woman to prefer the cloister to a vice-presidency."

I didn't know whether to believe him or not, but declined the offer, anyway. The last thing I needed or wanted were press notices.

That old ad agency of mine is still around, and it's much bigger than it was in my day. It could be that I contributed to its success and its climb into the big ten, for I did notice—in my final weeks there—that the rough language of the trade was not uttered in my presence, and for many years now the agency has represented (on a gratuitous basis) one of the huge national charities. Oh, yes, nuns do dream. And if the agency benefited from me, we are even, for I benefited from it. I learned many things of a promotional nature on Madison

Avenue that would come in handy during my future work as a sister.

There's not much more to relate about my prenovitiate days. The office party for me is worth mentioning, perhaps, because it was unusual for Madison Avenue: the hardest drink served was ginger ale. And the final shopping spree that left me almost penniless. And the last date with good friend Sam.

It all added up to the day in March when the six of us rode over the Hudson in a sea-green Ford.

2

The Bell of St. Michael's

If art mirrors life and Hollywood is art, then life in the novitiate was unreal.

But I found it real, and exhausting, and quite unlike a dozen
films I'd seen, wherein the long hours of every day were filled
with processions, confessions, prayers and tears, and very little
else. You were wrong, Hollywood, and you're still wrong. I
haven't found a novitiate featuring long corridors crammed
with statuary, pretty ponds with swans, acres of gardens, won-
drous fountains, and marble columns galore. And why do
the films always neglect the bell? That's really misleading the

41

young ladies in the audience. And not all the hopefuls in a novitiate are beautiful. Just the majority.

There were forty-four of us at St. Michael's on the first day of my new life there. Eleven postulants, including myself, and thirty-three novices of junior and senior grades. And for those who wonder (in Hollywood and elsewhere) about those simple terms: a postulant serves for six months, and if all goes well, she becomes a junior novice; after a year, if all goes well again, the junior becomes a senior novice and enjoys, for another year, such privileges as a private room with a real built-in closet and washstand, and first choice of toothpaste and soap brands.

Overseeing our activities were two sisters with the titles of Mistress of Novices and Assistant Mistress. We of the younger generation referred to them in our whispers as Sister Radar and Sister Junior Radar. Each of the dear souls possessed a 360-degree field of vision and could see through solid walls. They were adept at mind reading, too. Very little escaped their attention. Indeed, long before the popularity of bugging devices, Sister Radar would stand in the subbasement and detect precisely what was going on in the attic. There were those among us who insisted that He helped her at such times, and that may have been the case. There was no other easy explanation.

How she could suddenly appear on the third floor when everyone knew she was in her office on the first floor was easier to explain. The elevators were for the exclusive use of the resident and visiting sisters. We—postulants and novices alike —were required to trudge up and down the steep staircases.

I was the oldest of the postulants and the least naïve, and not an early believer in the super-powers of Sister Radar. I was more amused than impressed by the tales of her all-seeing and all-knowing talents.

I put her talents to the test on an afternoon in my third week. Already late for science class on the second floor and aware that both sisters were away from the building, I saved a few precious seconds by riding the staircase rail from the third floor to the second. Nobody witnessed the feat. I was all alone.

Following supper that evening, Sister Radar called me into her office. "Were you in the attic after hours last night, Sister Eleanor?" she asked.

"No, Sister."

"Then when did you get your riding boots?"

All of us had a personal trunk stored in the attic. The trunks held our lay clothes and personal treasures—the things we would need if we failed to make the grade or decided to leave. My trunk, of course, held bowling shoes and riding boots. So I answered, "My riding boots are still in the trunk, Sister. I didn't get them out."

"Well, you should have," she told me. "Always wear riding boots when you're riding, Sister Eleanor!" She smiled and added, "Get them out tonight. They'll protect your stockings during your additional busywork."

And so I became a believer.

For the next three weeks I mopped the classroom floors. All the classroom floors. Twice a day, wearing riding boots. I never rode the staircase rail again.

"Busywork" was the theme song of St. Michael's, and Sister didn't let us forget it. It meant keeping busy during every moment of one's wakeful hours. Despite the findings of medical research, the radar twins did not believe that rest periods recharged human batteries. It was go-go-go, sleep, then go-go-go again.

When, on a dare, I mentioned that Thomas Edison took frequent naps and that the very active Eleanor Roosevelt rested for ten minutes every few hours, I wished I had kept my big mouth shut. "We were aware of those facts when we turned down their applications," Sister Junior Radar informed me.

Sister Helen, the postulant who dared me, discovered a convincing way to avoid the always-at-work bit. She did it right out in the open by walking along with head bent and eyes cast toward the floor or ground. The expression on her face, the slight movement of her lips, and her slow pace increased the picture of a devout young lady lost in prayer. She developed this into a fine art. Then, fearful of overdoing it, she added a touch of variety by walking around in the same manner, but occupying her hands with sewing.

All of us were envious of Sister Helen's success. I think I might have copied her tactics, but I had little talent and absolutely no liking for sewing. The temptation to at least infringe on her praying copyright disappeared at the end of the second month: Sister Helen, complete with trunk and deposit, was sent home.

And then there were ten postulants, and all ten of us were suddenly anxious to go-go-go even more. We were settled in. So much so that we were no longer thinking of asking the Lord to melt the bell.

I think of that bell every time I see one or hear one, and I am sure I will do so for the rest of my life. I'm certain there's never been another one like it in this world. Somebody made it and then, bless him, broke the mold.

The bell of St. Michael's was located just outside the office door on the first floor. It didn't clang or peal or tinkle the way nice bells do. This one bellowed in a raucous tone. It sounded as loud in the attic as it did on the first floor, as if the architect of St. Michael's had worked overtime to assure perfect acoustics. I'll never know why my head didn't hit the ceiling of my cell on my first few mornings in the novitiate. The bell started our day.

It also ended our day and filled all the in-between hours with its never-varying clamor. Each shout was a command, directing us to drop what we were doing and to hurry elsewhere and do something else.

In a sense, the bell was our dictator, and we were its slaves. The fact that it was controlled by an electric clock, and thus was also a slave, didn't lessen our anti-bell feelings. We listened to that bell seven days a week, and all of us hoped for the day when its voice would be silenced for at least a short spell of time. These days, I like to think that our silent hopes broke through belatedly and He responded by producing that East Coast blackout of 1965. How I would have loved being back in St. Michael's on that great, silent-bell day! And I would have congratulated Sister Radar on her ability to see far into the future. In my day we used pocket watches, and we carried them at all times. Never have so many watches gone unwound. The bell told us the time of day.

It sounded first at five fifteen in the morning, commanding us to struggle from our beds and rush for the community facilities down the hall. Fifteen minutes later, the second bellow sent us scurrying down the stairs to the first-floor chapel for morning prayers. Each of us had her own special seat, and those of us who arrived late—or after prayers had begun—are still arriving late. Proof, if needed, that sisters are also the products of early environment.

It's hard to concentrate that early in the morning. One is barely awake, and most of us had not risen that early prior to entering the novitiate. It was enormously difficult for the novice appointed to lead the hour-long procession of morning prayers: prayers of the Office, for world peace, for the cures of cancer and other unsolved ills, for sisters around the world, for widows and orphans and all the needy, and for all those needing help and guidance, whether the knew it or not, everywhere. The prayers were bound to be repetitious, and by the third morning we could predict what prayers were coming next, and then it was most difficult to remain attentive, to say nothing of staying awake. But we did.

We all anticipated the six-thirty bell that summoned us from chapel for a half hour of meditation. This could be observed in private or in groups, but there weren't many groups in my time. I did some of my best meditating outdoors as I strolled around the grounds, combining deep thought with needed physical exercise.

Meditation was not a hit-or-miss proposition. Sister Radar gave us the subject, and quite often the subject was the virtues of St. Anthony. The library had many books on St. Anthony, and that may have been included in her reasoning. On such a morning I would walk around reading one of the books and thinking of his virtues, and try not to be critical of the dry, unimaginative writing or think of the virtues of another saint.

But on an average morning most of us headed for our cells. There we meditated and prayed, sitting in our straight-back chairs or kneeling at bedsides. Kneeling was safest, I suppose. We never knew when one of the good sisters would peek in the door, and it's easier to fall asleep in a chair. We were devout, but we were also human, and our tired bodies always fought our keen young minds that early in the day. The temptation to cheat a bit and steal a nap was great. After all, we'd just been through a whole hour of prayers that had seemingly covered every conceivable subject. How often I was tempted to pray for jockeys, ski instructors, breeders of horses, and owners of bowling alleys! They would have added variety and sustained my wakefulness. I managed to refrain.

Still, on a visit to St. Michael's years later, I did ask one of the sisters if such prayers would have been proper.

"Jockeys?" she replied. "Perhaps. But from what I have read, Sister, it would seem that bettors are more needy."

I felt relieved, and I didn't confess that I had taken care of them in prayers for my own father and his friends and their daily problems.

At seven, the bell called us to chapel again for Mass. And in response to its seven-thirty shout, we trooped down into the subbasement's dining room for breakfast. All meals were served there on tables arranged in a huge circle. The resident sisters had no need for their personal radars. We were all in their view, and heads were easy to count. Of course, there was no need for them to count. Now we were all awake, hungry, and present. Even the ones consistently late for everything were usually on time for breakfast.

Food was served family style. The postulants sat in a line. All chairs were assigned, and getting our share of the food was sometimes difficult, for several of the newcomers were not accustomed to passing along the platters. They would serve themselves and put the platter down out of reach of the next diner. Unfortunately, meals were consumed in silence. Since we couldn't speak, there was no way to pass the word along that some of us were being shortchanged. Those were the times for silent prayers, and sometimes, but not always, the prayers worked. The offender would remember her obligation to the rest of us and pass along the food.

Six days a week, breakfast consisted of fruit juice, dry cereal, toast, and eggs. On Sundays, sausages accompanied the eggs. I sometimes wonder if the poultry industry realizes that it is largely subsidized by the Church. If so, it might show its appreciation by adding a little flavor to eggs. I have nothing against eggs, really, except the memory of them—day after day after day.

The only voice heard in the dining room—at breakfast, dinner, and supper—was that of the postulant or novice assigned to the duty of reader. Again, she served for a week at a time, reading from the pages of books designated by Sister Radar. It was customary to read about the life of saints, and normally one read books about the saint whose name she hoped to take as her own. Since none of us had a priority on any given saint, there were always several with the identical choice. In my time as a postulant, three novices also favored St. Vincent de Paul, and had our breakfast reading assignments been continuous, we would have heard about him for twenty-eight breakfasts in a row. It would have been the identical words over and over again, for our material was limited to that in the novitiate's library. New books about saints aren't published every day.

In a given year we heard about St. Vincent and other saints

many times, but never for twenty-eight breakfasts in a row. But I recall what may have been a record—twenty-one meals in a row devoted to the life of St. Theresa. The sixteenth-century Spanish nun was more popular than my choice, and the luck of the draw (one reader for each meal) brought forth three novices who favored her in the same week and read from the same book. Ever since, whenever I've met a Sister Theresa, it seems to me that I've known her before.

The voice of the breakfast reader continued until it was drowned by the sound of the bell at eight sharp. We folded our napkins (one had to last for a week), placed them on the tables, and except for the few assigned to refectory cleanup, headed for our cells for bed-making and tidying the premises. Ten minutes were allotted for those duties and such other personal tasks as sewing or polishing shoes. But sewing was not my forte. I preferred gazing out the window, for it had a view of the Hudson and beyond. It was a secret, sentimental ritual. On a clear day I could see my old high school and Manhattan apartment houses where I'd partied. Every day I could see the Hudson and would remember Circle Line cruises with Sam. So almost every morning, between eight and eight ten, I wallowed in pleasant memories of the old days for just a few seconds. Nobody knew about those stolen seconds in the morning. Not even Sister Radar. Or if they did, they approved. I don't think it was the cause of any of my additional busywork.

At eight ten, the bell sent us off on a series of assignments that would last until noon, and it would sound off at thirty- and forty-minute intervals so that if we had memorized our schedules, we would be in the next place at the right time. Those morning hours were a mixture of work and higher education. Singly or in small groups, we would accomplish the chores: washing dishes, scrubbing, painting, dusting, cleaning windows, and beating rugs. Then we were off to history or Scripture class, and then back to housecleaning, then off again to science or math or language. The muscles were warmed first, then the minds. The rigors of suburbia and academia combined.

Some of the postulants found it a simple matter to slip into the daily routine, but it wasn't easy for me. Oh, the studies still came naturally, and I wasn't against labor so long as we all shared the tasks. It was the lack of person-to-person communication that bothered me most. I'd been talking my head off since my earliest days, and postulants weren't supposed to talk to postulants, or to novices, or to the sisters—unless the sisters opened the conversation, which was always brief. There seemed to be no established law against whispering, however, so sometimes I whispered, but hardly anyone ever whispered back. Even when we were obviously out of the audio range of the good sisters, nobody wanted to whisper back. I suppose the rest of them weren't born talkers.

It seems to me now that I practiced admirable restraint, but that is a personal view. Except for the good sisters, the other residents at St. Michael's referred to me as Windy. While the nickname was probably appropriate, it was based on a false premise. The postulant in the cell next to mine claimed I was so completely incapable of keeping my mouth closed that I talked continuously in my sleep. Two other nearby postulants could not verify this, but I was stuck with the sobriquet for the rest of my days at the novitiate, and it has surfaced many times since.

I'm sure that Sister Radar knew that I hadn't turned into a

silent mouse, but she never came right out and told me so. She made her point by assigning me, without always stating the reasons, to a multitude of additional busywork. Often the work was for her, as when she directed me to mend several pairs of her stockings, and I told her I had no talent for sewing or mending.

"We shall see," she said, as she handed me the stockings.

We did see, and when she looked over the results of my handiwork, she commented, "You are an honest woman, Sister." Never again did she ask me to sew for her, but in time I became her favorite typist and the conqueror of St. Michael's ancient, faulty mimeograph.

The noon bell sent us back to chapel for recitation of the psalms and an examination of conscience. Fortunately, these examinations were silent ones. Otherwise, every noon chapel would have been crucial. First I asked myself how I was doing. I always passed that one with flying colors. Then I asked myself if I was the same person I had been the day before, and the day before that, ad infinitum. Of course! Next, was I being honest about my private opinion of myself? Had I turned off the hot water in the third-floor sink? Would I have time to catch up on my mail this week? Oh, it was easy to run off the track.

Then the twelve-thirty dinner bell. The thirty-minute meal was the big one of the day. Hearty and healthy, but the cook wouldn't have found employment at Voisin. Soup, potato, vegetable, and meat, and the same linen napkin. Sometimes it was fowl instead of meat, and always it was fish on Friday. The menu was predictable, in that it was always the same on the day-of-the-week basis: Monday's fare was last Monday's, Tuesday's fare was always Tuesday's and would be the same next Tuesday. The only variation was on important religious occasions: turkey.

Still, we weren't there for the sole purpose of eating, and I stress the midday meal only because it was followed by an hour of recreation. This always took place outdoors, fair or foul weather, and we had our choice of several activities: basketball, softball, volleyball, badminton, and tennis. While silence was appreciated, person-to-person communications were not banned during recreation hour so long as remarks were pertinent and voices were kept low. I waited in vain for a blizzard, so that I could run outside and ask, "Tennis, anyone?"

Why recreation after a heavy meal? That still puzzles me after all these years. Body discipline, perhaps.

Whatever the reasoning, that dictator bell (yes, it penetrated stone walls and could be heard outdoors) called us indoors for two more hours of studies and classes. And at least once a week, the old finishing-school spirit would invade the novitiate for thirty afternoon minutes: lessons in voice and diction; or a lesson in poise, which never advanced much beyond walking around with a book atop one's head.

The bell at four o'clock was, for a change, a welcome sound. It meant a ten-minute coffee break and another chance to communicate. Since the Church was here first, Madison Avenue has borrowed at least this one idea from it. At St. Michael's, coffee break also meant tea, milk, and fruit juice, and sometimes cookies.

Then, from the end of the break until five, we were free to attend to personal things (mending, washing, reading, letters), but were also expected to toil at the piano, or the organ, or both. I happened to have ten thumbs, and never did advance beyond a poor rendition of "Pussycat" on the piano.

Those fifty minutes were also the time for the choir and the glee club to rehearse. It was impossible for both to rehearse on the same day, however, for twenty of the choir's twenty-five voices constituted the glee club. No solution was found.

It wasn't long before my deficiencies on the keyboard were noted by the sisters. While still a novice, I was put in charge of the entertainment that was performed for visitors on feast days. This was a wise and kind move on their part, for the duty provided me with ample excuse to use my vocal cords. Be sure that Sister Eleanor was mistress of ceremonies on every feast day, and that she also appeared in most of the original skits. Broadway never knew what it missed Off Broadway at St. Michael's.

Five to six was spent in busywork, if assigned, or spiritual reading, individually or in groups. And six o'clock meant supper: cold cuts or sardines, bread, cheese, pickles once in a while, coffee or milk. Then busywork until seven thirty.

It was probably the only time I stole a look at my pocket watch. With a great stretch of the imagination, one could detect a mellow undertone in the bell's next shout. It brought us all together for a solid hour of relaxation. The rules specified that we had to sew, but we could also talk, although the talk was not supposed to descend to the level of gossip. And if something of the utmost importance was happening in the world, the sisters might turn on the television or the radio. But nothing much of importance ever seemed to happen, so those treats were rare. It wasn't a prime time for the broadcasting of important events, anyway.

After that prized hour, the bell sounded in rapid sequence:

Eight thirty. Down to chapel for night prayers and to say good night to the Lord.

Eight forty-five. To the dining room for a hot drink. Nine times out of ten it was gruel, and almost always awful. It was not possible to skip this treat. Sister Radar had an interesting theory about the benefits derived from drinking something hot at this time of night, although she did not indulge. "Without it, you will fade away," she insisted. The gruel was always served red-hot, even on the warmest nights of summer. Then off to our cells. A fast five minutes.

Eight fifty. The bell sounded for the last time. Room Night Silence was in effect. We were not supposed to talk or to whisper. Not even to ourselves. It was a needless rule, in a way. We were so tired. All of us were so very, very tired. We welcomed the time for final prayer and sleep.

Still, there were nights when I stood by my window for a long time, looking across the Hudson to Fun City's flickering lights, watching the moving lights on the George Washington Bridge and the dancing lights on the river.

On one such night, I heard the door to my cell open. I turned and saw Sister Radar.

"Something wrong, Sister Eleanor?" she asked.

"No, Sister."

"Just memories?"

"Yes, Sister."

"We all have them, Sister Eleanor. Hold on to them. The good ones, anyway."

"I will, Sister. Thank you."

"It's a human trait, you see," she continued. "You and I

54

are humans, Sister Eleanor. Not superior to others, but just plain human beings. You understand?"

I nodded, and as she closed the door, she said, "Your first busywork in the morning will be to place your bed by the window."

I didn't wait until morning. I did it that very night. And was wide awake and ready for action when the bell sounded again at five fifteen.

So, Hollywood, that's the way it was in the novitiate. The day started and ended with a bell, and not a single postulate or novice went to the office to say, "I have a problem, Sister. Last night, a brick flew through my window, and a note was attached to it, and the note was from Harold. I'm sorry I can't show you the note because I was so ashamed that I swallowed it, but here's the brick. May I go home, Sister? Harold has a new Caddy and he needs me."

It could be that the big thinkers in Beverly Hills invented such nonsense for their story lines because it was impossible to build an interesting plot based on truth. I can't recall a single postulant who crossed the bridge because of a broken heart, or as a means to personal security, or as an escape from the world's confusions and troubles. Rather, all hoped to find in this new life a ways and means to help the world.

The girls who entered the novitiate were not colorful characters, although they came from all walks of life and different levels of experience and background. Each was a personality, yes, but it took the good sisters no more than a day to blend all the diverse personalities into a single, uniform one that could have been termed the St. Michael's Type.

The type was obedient. Busywork was our theme, the bell was our dictator, and obedience was our hallmark. We listened, we obeyed, and we did not ask questions. I still don't know why our hands had to be piously concealed when we were not occupied with some worthy task. "The high cost of soap, perhaps?" whispered Kelly on a Sunday afternoon. We were walking along the bank of the Hudson, a full half mile from the novitiate. If she had screamed, I alone would have heard her; but she whispered out of obedient habit. Twice a week, on Wednesday and Sunday afternoons, we were free to leave the novitiate for two hours. There was no sense in window-shopping, for none of us had a penny. So we took walks, and oddly—since we were free to talk—didn't talk very much.

And our pace, even free of the novitiate, was the same as the one we maintained so diligently inside the stone walls. One step after the other. Not too slow, not too fast, and always noiseless. There's nothing as habit-forming as obedience.

None of us ever inquired why it was necessary—alone or in public view—to sit ramrod upright at all times, and with our backs free of any material support. The mastering of obedient sitting would have been easier if the furnishings had been plain stools instead of chairs and benches. In time, our spinal columns adjusted to the ruling, and to this day many of us sit on the edge of our chairs.

Hands, steps, voices, backs, walking, sitting, kneeling—a great deal of time, concentration, and supervision were spent on such externalisms. Their importance was never revealed, but we suspected that somehow they pushed us along the road to true holiness. Again, none of us asked the reasons, and if we had, perhaps the Radar sisters couldn't have answered. Things had been that way for a long time, and there was no clairvoyant among us to predict that things would ever change, or—as a recent lecturer put it—that "a round little Italian named John would come along."

The only hint I can recall came from Sister Radar, and even in that case I may be retrospectively reading between the lines. I had not been called to her office for a good two weeks, an uncommonly lucky span of time for me, so I wasn't surprised when a summons came, although I wondered which of my nonobedient activities had been observed. My missing watch? I had lost it somewhere in the novitiate during the preceding week.

"Sister Eleanor, do you happen to know a good friend of ours from Newark?" was the sister's greeting. "Thomas J. Walden, who seems to be in the soap business?"

I couldn't remember anyone named Walden.

"Well, unless somebody made a mistake, Mr. Walden thinks very highly of you. We have received twenty cartons of hand soap from him, including the two brands most favored by the senior novices. Now, as to the mistake, if it was one, please examine the contents of the carton on the chair."

It was a small cardboard carton, and it contained two dozen round, flat cans of Propert's, every horse lover's idea saddle soap.

"You may take three cans for use on your riding boots, Sister Eleanor. Take the other cans to the supply closet."

I almost forgot to thank her. A pocket watch was resting face-up on a small table next to the carton of saddle soap. The watch was the only object on the table. She wanted me to see it, but I didn't dare ask if it was mine, and if so, where she had found it. So all I said was, "Thank you, Sister. Will that be all?"

"Almost. I want you to list all the leather-bound volumes in the library. Many of the bindings are in very poor condition, but I'm sure that elbow grease and saddle soap will revive them. This task will constitute your additional busywork, effective immediately. I don't think it will take you more than a month, providing you use your free afternoons. That will be all, Sister Eleanor."

And then, as I moved toward the door, she said, "Speaking of bowling shoes, Sister Eleanor"—and we had not been speaking about bowling shoes—"what about it?"

I was puzzled. "It?" I asked.

"Bowling, I mean. Young ladies didn't bowl in my time. Tell me about it."

It seemed a strange request, but I was happy to oblige, and it may have been the only time one of her charges contributed to her education. When my five-minute lecture ended, she nodded her thanks and dismissed me with a wave of one hand. Carrying the carton of saddle soap, I marched up the stairs to the second floor and proceeded to the supply closet.

The supply closet was opened once a week: just before supper on Saturday. It held our personal needs: soap, toothpaste, sheets, pillow slips, and minor medicines. We could talk freely as we waited in line, so long as the talk was restricted to classroom studies. This wasn't a Saturday, but I was sure the supply closet would be open.

Sure enough, a senior novice was waiting for me. I handed her the carton. She removed three cans from the carton, gave them to me, then stored the rest in the closet and locked the door. No words were exchanged. Then I did a military about-face and headed for the attic, where I stored the three cans in my trunk and whispered words of reassurance to my riding boots. From there, I marched down four flights of stairs to the library, where—not unexpectedly—the same senior novice was waiting for me. She departed as soon as I started listing the leather-bound volumes that would weary my arms during the coming weeks. I was being obedient to the final T.

During the supper hour a few days later, Sister Radar announced that a pocket watch had been found. "I am sorry to say that the watch was found on an elevator," she added, and if we had been permitted to gasp, then gasps would have filled every square inch of the room. We all knew that the elevators were out-of-bounds and for the exclusive use of the sisters—the two resident sisters and the visiting sisters who conducted our classes. It was a major rule of obedience that no candidate in her right mind would ever break. "Will the candidate who lost her watch in the elevator please stand?"

I had been riding one of the elevators off and on for several weeks. I had ridden unobserved, even when a sister was on the elevator. It was not a feat of magic on my part, but just some clever thinking: I hid myself in the huge wicker laundry hamper; it was a good four feet high and over two feet wide, plenty of room for a crouching novice.

Obviously, I had somehow dropped the watch in that hamper and somebody in the laundry room had discovered it. And while all our watches were identical, each carried the owner's initials on the back—a fact that I hadn't forgotten.

So I stood and received yet another summons to the office. I was frightened that time and almost sure that the recent meal had been a last supper at the novitiate for me. Both sisters were present, and that hadn't happened before. I stood before them, remembering to conceal my hands, and also to cross my fingers.

"When I was a little girl, Sister Eleanor," Sister Radar began, "I was sent to my room because of poor table manners and told to finish my dinner there. When my mother checked on me, she found that I had climbed out the window and was eating dinner on the porch roof. She scolded me, and I thought she was unjust, for I had obeyed her in going to my room, and she said nothing about the roof. Now, Sister, are you going to tell me that you were not riding on the elevator, but that you were riding in a hamper which happened to be on an elevator, and there's no rule about that?"

"No, Sister."

"Am I going to look up someday and see you climbing around on the roof of St. Michael's simply because I have not ruled the roof out-of-bounds?"

"No, Sister."

She motioned to me to sit, so I sat—stiffly upright on the very edge of the chair with my back at least twelve inches from the chair's back. My facial expression must have been serious, for I was truly worried now, convinced that I had been judged a failure, and that I had been directed to sit only to save me from falling.

"We have reached an interesting conclusion. Of all the candidates, you are the only one with fear in her heart. You are afraid that in the process of becoming a nun, you will somehow lose your personal identity. Now, look at me, Sister Eleanor. Whether you approve of it or not, would you say that I lacked a personality of my own? Would you say that I am not a human being in my own right? Do you think my ecclesiastical training—the same as we have here at St. Michael's, by the way—destroyed me as an individual?" She paused, then she smiled as she said, "I think our relationship will be happier if you don't answer those questions, Sister Eleanor. You will spend tomorrow afternoon in prayer, contemplation, and self-appraisal. This time, you will decide to remain or retire. If there is a next time, I will decide. Take your watch. That's all."

The next day was a Wednesday. I spent the free hours in the solitude of my cell, praying and contemplating and self-appraising over and over again, although not always in that order, and sometimes speculating about where the others might be walking on that pleasant, sunny day. There was never any doubt in my mind about remaining. Then, as before and now, a dedicated Quin was a Quin dedicated. I did question the good sister's accusation that my flaunting of certain obedience rules meant that I was fighting to retain my personal identity, but in the end I had to agree. A Quin was a Quin, and I had been acting like Miss Misconduct all over again, but this time in the wrong place. So I dedicated myself to being as obedient as my nature would permit, and to the avoidance of pleasures that were not permitted, however attractive.

I figured my chances of remaining were a little less than those of the other candidates, or about at the 70 percent level. Or it could have been 75 percent. I wasn't indispensable, but nobody else could keep that mimeo machine in working order.

Still, I worried through all the rest of my days at St. Michael's, and never felt really secure. I had an eye for temptation, and it had both its eyes on me. Blind obedience had its place in the scheme of things, so long as it didn't get too personal.

The feeling of absolute security didn't come. Not even when Sister Judith, our Latin teacher, departed for a new assignment in the Philippines, and I became her temporary replacement. Later, the temporary status became permanent, and I was a forty-minute faculty member, five days a week. I was the only novice teaching her contemporaries.

It was a great honor, but I still couldn't ride the elevators. When I requested this special dispensation, it was vetoed in a hurry:

"The likes of you may be right in the long run, Sister Eleanor, but for the present, we'll continue to do things my way," said Sister Radar.

I think she did see into the future.

O nce in a while, but not often enough, I've found the time for brief visits at St. Michael's. Whenever I do go back, I remember the terrible fire that turned the night into red daylight and destroyed the building next door.

It had been St. Joseph's Home for Boys, and its boys—most of them orphans—belonged to the same community as the novitiate: the Sisters of St. Joseph of Newark. So the home and the novitiate were related, but not in activities.

In my days as a novice, the boys presented one of the greatest temptations for breaking the mandate of silence. It would happen in spring, when the boys were playing softball outdoors, and an obviously unfair decision would be made on the field. Standing there watching, I'd bite my lip to keep from shouting, "Kill the umpire!" I think such a shout would have ended me as a novice. The umpire was always either a sister or a priest.

No lives were lost in the fire, and the home was never re-built. Temporary quarters were found for the boys, none of them older than fifteen.

The fire occurred just two months before I graduated from the novitiate. It started a chain of events that would directly involve my own future, but I didn't know that at the time.

So the building isn't there anymore, and it hasn't been for years. Grass has replaced it. That's one change that's happened since my days at the novitiate, and there have been others:

The bell of St. Michael's doesn't sound off anymore! Silencing it was the first of the new freedoms put into effect, and generations of future novices should be grateful.

"Actually, it was the second thing I did," Sister Radar once told me. "When Pope John opened the window, I stood by it and breathed the fresh air, and then I silenced the bell. Think of it. All these years! No wonder I'm tone deaf. I left it there so that it can repent for all those years."

"Any other big changes?" I asked.

"A few, a few," she chuckled. "As you know, I'm not one to rush into things. How long has it been since you were here under my command, Sister Vincent? Fifteen years?"

"And you still drive the same sedan. I saw it outside."

She nodded and glanced at her watch. "Postulants never change. Just can't hurry them. That girl has been washing my car for over an hour. Does it every Saturday for me. She's fond of antiques."

The postulant washing the car was barefoot and wearing shorts. I commented on her attire.

"The new ones are much more practical than in your day," I was told. "I can still see you mopping floors in your long skirt and riding boots. Oh, Sister Ruth!"

Ruth Wilson, a junior novice, did an abrupt right turn and entered the office. She was dressed in a tailored suit and made no attempt to conceal her hands. "Yes, Sister?"

"How did it go?"

"I think I have the job. I'll know for sure on Tuesday."

"Fine. This is Sister Vincent dePaul. She is the reason for many of my gray hairs. Will you please show her your cell, for once it was her cell, and beware of her questions. Now I have a great many letters to dictate. Drop in before you leave, Sister."

"Stairs or elevator?" asked Ruth as we walked down the hallway. An unnecessary question. We rode the elevator to the third floor. These days, only the postulants walk. The novices have a choice, so they ride.

The door to my old cell gave me quite a start. It was the same old door, and in my day not even a scratch had been permitted to show. On this day it sported a bold red and white sign: *Simon & Garfunkel*. The cell's two solid walls, once spotless and barren, displayed a travel poster dedicated to the glories of Spain, a magazine cover featuring Eugene McCarthy, and an old photograph of the Wilson family (with the novice sitting on her father's knee). The curtained walls were covered with college pennants, including those of Yale and Cornell. The old straight-back chair was there, but an easy chair and a night table had been added. A transistor radio, with earphones attached, stood on the table; how the nights had changed! There was a neat stack of paperbacks (popular titles) on the bureau, and the mirror above was a vast improvement on the old hand one I'd struggled with for so long. The bedspread was of many colors, and they hid the creases that had been considered the next things to sin when they showed on the white ones of my time (and I had solved the problem by placing scapular boards under the mattress). The view from the window was just about the same. Otherwise, the square footage wasn't reminiscent of my old cell.

The novitiate's cells aren't really cells anymore. Neater and cleaner and smaller than the rooms in college dormitories, perhaps, but otherwise much the same. It wouldn't be quite right to state that the old college spirit has invaded the novitiate, but certainly the new freedoms are there. Indeed, many of today's novices come straight from college campuses, often with degrees. This means that the average postulant is now a bit older, certainly more mature, and surer of her dedication. And today dedication isn't always enough. All candidates undergo intensive screening, including psychological tests. A little less than half of the hopefuls are accepted, and of these the percentage of failures and dropouts is negligible. Thus it's reasonable to assume that the qualities of today's postulants are higher than ever before in Church history, and if the end result doesn't benefit the world, then we'll have to devise new tests. I, for one, don't fret about that. The dedication of our new nuns is no less than before, and their ambitions are soaring.

Ruth Wilson, my tour director, was a fine example of the new crop. A graduate of Boston University, she had every intention of earning her M.A. at Columbia through summer courses, and may have done so by now. She was a year away from starting when I saw her on a day in June, but others from the novitiate were already on campuses and earning credits toward their degrees. These days, the novitiate encourages novices to continue their educations, although the number doing so is still limited by available funds. The funds come from the savings of other novices who live out, so to speak, during the summer months, while working away on salaried jobs. Nine months at the novitiate, three months at work or study, then back to the novitiate again: that's the new system. How I would have loved it!

The new occupant of my old cell was twentieth century all the way. She had chosen the religious life for reasons she couldn't precisely define—a not unusual state of mind—and over the objections of her family. "I didn't like the way the world was going," she explained, "and I suppose this seemed the best way for me to be of some help to others." She glanced at the college pennants, laughed, and continued, "Yale still writes that he can't live without me. He's now in the process of divorcing his second wife. I think he'll survive." Then she was silent for a long moment before asking, "Are you in the habit of giving novices advice?"

"It depends," I said. "I do if I feel that I'm qualified."

"Well, I know you didn't wear lay clothes at all when you were here, but we do, and it poses a social problem in the outside world. Several men have asked me for dates, and I suppose it will happen again. It's sort of embarrassing, explaining who I am and why I can't date. It's something we all run into. How would you handle it?"

Happily, I was qualified to give her the proper advice. Indeed, it was tested advice, for it had already worked for some of the young nuns at my convent. "Clasp your hands to the fore," I told Ruth, "then gaze demurely at your shoe tops and respond with these words: 'Kind Sir, I thank you, but I am dedicated.' It stops them every time. They may not understand, but it always stops them. Sister Alice used the words several times at Jones Beach last Saturday. They seem more effective when one is wearing a bathing suit."

We chatted for a good half hour, reviewing the old days and comparing them to the new. The hours are just as long and the basic schedule is much the same at St. Michael's, but things are dramatically different on the surface. Except for designated times, the choice of attire is up to the girls: novitiate habit or lay. Freedom of speech has arrived, and talking is even permitted at meals. Mail—incoming and outgoing—is no longer censored, and no one dictates the choice of radio and television programs. The famous readers at mealtime belong to the past, so dining is really a relaxed, social affair, and paper napkins have replaced the old once-a-week linen ones that had to be kept clean and folded just so. And today, the lights go out at night when the individual desires. So many changes! This one novitiate is keeping in step with the world, and so are most of the others around the land. Those that haven't changed, or don't intend to change, may have to fold their tents for lack of candidates. This is the age of thinking young women, and they're joining the fold not to find a private sanctuary, but to become a part of the action.

I declined an invitation to visit my old private room on the fourth floor. It had been mine during my term as a senior novice, and I wanted to remember it as it had been. For all I knew, it might be home to a color television set, and I didn't have one of those at the convent.

Sister Radar was waiting for me in her office. "Stop gawking and sit down!" she ordered.

I was staring with good reason. Her hair was pure white. I had never seen it before. And she had changed from her long habit to a light linen suit and blouse.

"For your information, I'm dining out with friends this evening, and then we're going to the theater. And this suit is not a Dior. I made it myself, with the help of about six novices. We found the pattern in some silly magazine. Tell me, did you ever learn to sew?"

I told her no, and wondered if the secret of the black veil hadn't really been a secret to her. If so, now was the moment for her to reveal that I hadn't deceived her, but all she said was, "The Lord must have inspired you that one time. Do you remember?"

I nodded. How could I forget that awful Wednesday, ten days before we senior novices were due to become professed sisters, when Sister Junior Radar announced that Sister Mary would be on hand at five thirty to inspect the long black veils we would wear? Each of us had been ordered to make her own veil, and it was, of course, an impossible assignment for me. The meticulous Sister Mary demanded perfection in all things, and I had planned to please her with a work of art that Frances Smith's mother had made for me. The only trouble with the plan was that I hadn't received the veil. Delivery had been arranged for the next Saturday afternoon, a full day before the previously announced inspection time.

So I was caught veilless on that Wednesday, and the situation called for some quick thinking. The name of Quin was first on the inspection list, and down in ninth place was Brandon, easily the queen of the needle-and-thread set at St. Michael's. Brandon owed me a favor, for she was weak in Latin, and I had constantly granted her higher grades than she deserved. So she was hardly in a position to deny me the loan of her veil.

At the appointed hour, I presented this veil to Sister Mary, and it passed her rigid inspection with flying colors. But she had warmed to her task when she got down to the ninth (or very same) veil, however, and found that it contained all sorts of flaws. Brandon was ordered to rip it apart and start all over again on a new veil. My savior was in tears when she returned to her room.

"And what did you think of Sister Ruth?" asked Sister Radar, bringing me back to the present.

"I liked her. She's very outgoing."

"Yes. And it might interest you to know, Sister, that her cell was given her for old times' sake. The others call her Windy. Did she tell you about the summer job she hopes to acquire?"

"No. Advertising?"

"Real estate. It's her father's business, so she knows something about it. She tells me that she'll earn a fortune in commissions by bringing truth to the field. Calling a mud hole a mud hole and not a pond, and not misrepresenting a shack on a lot as an estate. Now you know all about making money, so is this the right approach?" I had no time to reply, for she was off and running with, "As soon as I saw Sister Ruth's psychological test, I knew we had a winner. The first question asked what one would rather be doing than taking the test. Most of the time, the answer is praying in chapel or out helping the needy. She wrote that she'd rather be playing tennis. An honest woman. I suppose your answer would have been bowling. No, I haven't tried it myself as yet, but who knows?"

Age has nothing to do, really, with a nun's acceptance of her new and largely undefined liberties. She may prove to be the most adaptable woman on earth. Almost overnight, her role has changed from that of a respected mystique to that of an average contributing member to all of society. A few of the old-schoolers, if that's the proper terminology, do find the transition difficult, for it's not easy to shed the traditions of a lifetime. It's as if they feel their privacy has been invaded, and while they accept the new ways, they find it difficult to embrace them. But don't count Sister Radar among them.

"I find that I prefer wearing lay clothes when I'm on the outside," she confessed. "They seem to symbolize that I'm really a part of this world and serve to remind me that I'm not a special sort of person. The only drawback comes when I'm driving. All the other cars on the road seem to be aimed at mine. I feel safer when I'm wearing the habit. Then, somehow, even the wildest drivers try to avoid hitting me." The car she drove, if anyone's wondering, was not her personal property. It belonged to the community. And the car I drive belongs to my convent. It was a gift from a ladies' organization and purchased with funds raised under the campaign banner of Keep Sister Vincent on Wheels.

A copy of that day's *New York Times* was on her desk. Face-up was the first page of the second section. I had read it earlier, for it featured an interview with yet another priest who had left the Church to marry. Obviously, Sister Radar had read the story, too. Now she caught me glancing at the paper and asked, "What do you think of it?"

"It's happened before, it will happen again."

"I pity them," she commented. "I really do. I pity them.

Oh, I don't mean the priests. I mean the women they marry."

"Oh?"

"Now, Sister Vincent, don't look so surprised. You know very well what I mean. Some priests are spoiled men. Why, everything is done for them. The average one doesn't know how to boil water. I hope for their sakes that they marry patient women. And how about you? And what happened about the horses this year?"

I knew what she meant. As for me, I knew long before I entered the novitiate that marriage was not for me, and I haven't changed my mind since. I told her that, and there was no need to tell her what the public doesn't seem to know: a nun is free to leave the convent at any time and without risk of excommunication. All it takes is a simple letter to the Vatican, stating her intentions and requesting a release from her final vows. There are no handy statistics, but some nuns do write the letter and do leave the Church for marriage every year. Someday, perhaps, *The Times* will grant nuns equal space. Then, perhaps, we'll know whether it's proper to pity their husbands.

As for the horses, my love for them had remained and inspired a fine fund-raising device: the horse show. The overhead involved in sponsoring an outdoor horse show is never a minor matter, but the public's response via the box office had always been tremendous. In the first three years of our annual shows, we netted close to a hundred thousand dollars for the benefit of St. Joseph's Village for Dependent Children. The shows were for a worthy cause, of course, but that didn't seem to matter on the day of the fourth show. The heavens donated buckets of rain from dawn to late afternoon. The horses didn't mind, nor did the owners and riders, but the public stayed home. Would it be proper to state that we nuns lost our shirts? Proper or not, we did. The dollar disaster influenced our thinking: no more horse shows. Too risky.

"You prayed for fair weather, of course, or were you over-confident?" asked Sister Radar.

"We prayed for weeks," I assured her.

"Just you?"

"All of us. Never have so many nuns prayed for fair weather."

"Then I can't understand what happened. Why would He object to a horse show?"

None of us is sure that He does, of course, although as time goes on the view becomes more firmly established. We've looked high and low for indoor space in New Jersey and never found it.

"I still have a few things to do," said Sister Radar by way of dismissal. "But before you leave, and speaking of horses, do you remember your parting words to me on the day you became a nun? Something like 'Put this to good use,' as you handed me a hundred and fifty dollars. You can be sure that I did put it to good use. And now, after all these years, I think I could stand the shock if you confessed that somehow you had managed to place a bet on a horse and had won. Am I right?"

She was wrong on both counts. The sum had been a hundred and sixty dollars, or twenty times eight dollars—the eight dollars being the sum Marie had been able to raise for my earrings and class ring. My five friends had made good on the bet we had made thirty months before the day I became a sister.

Of the five, only Frances had been present in the chapel for the ceremony. Her mother was there, too, but not my father. I hadn't heard from him in over two years. My brother wasn't there, either, but he'd written to explain that he couldn't break free from business to come East.

"You certainly had unlimited faith in yourself," said Frances, as she handed me the money. "My, Sister Vincent, what an attractive veil. Don't you think so, Mother?"

"A work of art, Sister Vincent."

My only other gift on that day was a telegram from Marie, the girl who had been so sure that she would never marry. She had sent it from a hospital, and it read: SORRY NOT PRESENT. BABY BOY BORN YESTERDAY. WE ARE NAMING HIM VINCENT. BLESS YOU. LOVE, MARIE.

3

The Temporary Nun

July 1953. I was no longer a senior novice named Sister Eleanor. I had become Sister M. Vincent dePaul Quin. A junior professed nun.

Or a temporary nun, as my friend Frances often called me. She was splitting hairs, really, and basing her reasoning on the fact that I would not take my final vows of poverty, chastity, and obedience for another three years. To the layman, this time span has always been something of a mystery, but to the nun it is no more or less than logic. The thirty-six months are devoted to both duty and great introspection, and during them she learns with absolute certainty about the depth of her desire to spend the rest of her life in His service. In a way, it is a time for proving oneself to self, and in another way, it is a time for proving oneself to God. But no matter how one regards it, the time span represents the last simple opportunity to turn away. Very few do. I recall only one of my contemporaries who did so, and in a general sense she remained in God's service, for she became a nurse.

It's all changed now, but in my day junior nuns weren't offered a choice of assignments. Others decided where we could best serve, and there was no possible way for any of us to state our preferences. This firm rule was not a deterrent to private hope, of course, and I spent my final weeks as a senior novice hoping that my first assignment would be with a mission in the Philippines. I was ready and willing to see a bit of the world, and my best friend among the professed nuns was already serving on Luzon. We had been corresponding, so she shared my hope, and both of us were backing the hope with prayers. Catholics like to believe that all prayers are favorably received and eventually fulfilled. We know better, of course, for there are scoundrels among us who pray for impossible things. Still, I was confident of success, for both the hope and the prayers had been shuttling back and forth over a big continent and a huge ocean for many months.

If overconfidence is a sin, then I was a sinner. I was assigned to St. Joseph's Home in Jersey City. The distance from the novitiate in Englewood Cliffs was and remains approximately eighteen miles. A modest journey at best, and a little disappointing in view of my many earnest prayers for world travel. But I accepted His decision as a lesson in humility.

The Home was a brownstone building with iron rails that had stood there for more than a century, facing a busy street and crowded on three sides by a complex of factory buildings owned by a manufacturer of name-brand toothpaste. I was not one to be intimidated by toothpaste, but for a long time I would suffer different versions of the same dream: something had gone wrong next door, and thirty-seven good sisters were swimming for their lives through a sea of toothpaste.

As the newcomer, and in point of seniority, I was the youngest sister in St. Joseph's. My feelings were those of a tenderfoot Brownie among real Girl Scouts for the first time, and I was treated as such. For scores of weeks I sat at the far end of the dining-room table and watched the slow progress of the huge lamb-chop platter. All I could do was sit there with a forced smile on my face and hope that the cook had counted portions correctly and pray that some senior sister wouldn't be overly hungry. And I wondered if, by the time I got to the top of the table, I'd be too old to enjoy the meat.

My room was private, but much smaller than the last one I'd called my own at the novitiate. It was just big enough to hold a bed, a chair, and a towel rack. And the view from the single window was a far cry from the one of the scenic Hudson that I'd been enjoying for two and a half years. Now the view was of a firehouse across the street. I think that it may have been older than St. Joseph's. It was not an attractive building, but it served its purpose. Before midnight, we hardly heard the fire engines when they sped to their destinations.

But when all the lights were out in St. Joseph's, motors roared and bells clanged and sirens screamed. The sirens never failed to awaken me, and often they saved me from "drowning in toothpaste."

But even when there was an absence of fires, the firehouse was never really quiet. Seven nights a week, in all seasons and in any sort of weather short of a blizzard, a man named Joe would settle down in a chair outside the firehouse and talk the night away. He worked there, but if he was a fireman he was an inactive one, for he never went to the fires. He seemed to spend most of his time talking to his associates, or to friends or strangers who came walking down the street. Joe's booming voice penetrated all the rooms facing the street. Unless one wanted to suffocate, there was no escape.

In all my years at St. Joseph's, I never did learn his surname. We dubbed him Joe Winchell. Not because of his voice, but because of his opinions on all subjects known to man. Often, when no lights were showing in our home, he broadcast his opinion of the good sisters who lived across the street. In his opinion, there was something wrong with a woman who didn't marry. We thought this rather odd, for we already knew—thanks to previous Joe Winchell broadcasts that we had been unable to turn off—that the authority was a confirmed bachelor. One night several of us heard him say, "Don't tell me anything about nuns! My own mother's sister was one. She used to stand on street corners, even in the rain and snow, playing a horn with the band!" After that, none of us was offended by his remarks.

But Joe's vocabulary went beyond Webster, and to fully understand some of his vocal essays would have required long years before the mast. The thirty-seven were not unduly disturbed, for we were adults and his choice of words bounced off us. But St. Joseph's Home was part orphanage, all the resident orphans were little girls, and not all of them were sound sleepers. Every so often, one of the little ones would be overheard using a word that had not been made in heaven. "It's my turn to play on the ———— swing!" for example.

Finally, I was assigned the task of doing something about Joe. "Be sure to use tact. We know he's a bit odd, but he may consider himself a good Christian. I'm sorry about this, but now we know prayers won't work, and you are so proficient at public relations." Those were my instructions from the Mother Superior, the only one I've ever known who considered that day lost when she didn't read *The Christian Science Monitor* and *The Wall Street Journal*.

It was my first important assignment, so I gave it considerable thought. Success meant that I would no longer be considered a Brownie.

"When you have a complaint, go to the head of the class," my father often told me. "That's the way to get action." He told it to my mother, too, but she remained unimpressed. When she felt that she had not received fair value for her money, or felt that a purchased item had been falsely represented, she was quite willing to speak her piece to the branch manager, but just wouldn't write a letter to the president of the A&P. She never received a penny's worth of satisfaction from any branch manager.

So I marched to City Hall and called upon the head of the class, or the mayor of Jersey City, New Jersey. I requested a few minutes of his valuable time, but the mayor was too busy to see anyone. I saw him through an open door, however, and he didn't look busy to me. So I pleaded, but to no avail. It was not an election year.*

The fire department was next. The chief was in Atlantic City. A Convention, not a fire. Nonetheless, I told the story of Joe to several intelligent-looking young men in the department. They were polite and amused, but none was sure that anything could be done about Joe what's his name. I understood. After all, Joe was not a fire.

Discouraged but not willing to concede defeat, I found my way to the department of sanitation and my strongest political contact: a stenographer who spent a great deal of her free time working as a volunteer at the orphanage. I told the story of Joe to her. "So where do I go from here?"

"Nowhere," she replied. "I'll take care of it. What's his full name?"

"I don't know."

"Well, that doesn't matter. Now forget all about it."

"If you don't mind," I asked, "how do you intend to take care of Joe?"

"Well, I'll tell my boss and he'll handle it. He's a Baptist and he has a thing about dirty words. The cleanest speech in City Hall is heard in Sanitation."

My report to Mother Superior was optimistic, if ambiguous. "Sister Vincent has taken care of the little matter across the way," she announced at dinner that night. All the senior

---

* Yes, we do vote and always have. That may come as news to many people. And we vote with conscientious regularity. While our numbers will never swing a national election, no other single calling or profession responds so fully to the American way of deciding who will govern.

sisters nodded and smiled, and there were enough sandwiches remaining for ten people when the platter reached me. I enjoyed a hearty meal. And later, as we discussed the day's events in the parlor, I dropped a few remarks designed to emphasize the fact that the cleansing of Joe might take a little time.

He was in his usual form that night and the next, and I wondered if another visit to Sanitation was in order. Then came a personal telephone call to Mother Superior from the fire chief. The man was full of apologies. He was just back from his convention and promised that Joe would be his first order of business. "I presume," she told me, "that he will attend to any fires later. You must have very strong connections."

From that night onward, Joe's volume was less and the words he employed were mostly pure. But he still resented us, and when summer came he had a phonograph for company and together they filled the early morning hours with music. Night after night, we were awakened by—or fell asleep to— the recorded notes of a little ditty called "Fascination." Joe would play the song over and over, as many as twenty times in a row. To this day I don't know what was on the other side of the record. He never played it. But I knew when the nightly serenade was coming to an end, for Joe always joined the feminine vocalist on the last two or three playings. We didn't appreciate this at first, but we did after the record had become very scratchy. And then, just as I was about to call on the help of Sanitation again, a little miracle happened: Joe disappeared.

He returned to his old stand three weeks later, but with a difference: no more phonograph, no more loud dissertations. He was a changed man. Joe Winchell, we learned, had married. Blessed be that woman. From then on our sleep was not disturbed at St. Joseph's, except for the sirens, bells, and brakes. Still, those sounds were easier on the eardrums than "Fascination."

But at St. Joseph's I was credited with the silencing of the man, and accepted as the sister with political influence. Mother Superior was the first to grant me such status.

"We're in trouble, we just don't have the money, honesty is the best policy and you know it as well as I, so I must ask your help," she informed me.

We were in trouble, almost a thousand dollars' worth of trouble, and it was the telephone company that was unaware that honesty is the best policy. It happened in this manner:

Our monthly telephone bill fluctuated between a low of forty dollars and a high of seventy-five dollars. The amount depended upon the number of toll charges incurred for business calls in behalf of the convent, orphanage, and other business. But in one particular month, the bill for St. Joseph's came to a record but accurate low of twelve dollars and eighty cents. To our amazement, the bill for the next month was for the same amount. We thought that was very nice and did not complain. And then, month by month, our admiration for the telephone company increased. For the next seventeen months, the bill was always the same: twelve dollars and eighty cents. It didn't make any difference how many long-distance calls were made—ten or a hundred and ten—the bill never varied. We suspected that something was wrong, of course, but we were also willing to believe that generous, kindly, all-loving people worked for the telephone company. They understood our many needs and appreciated our efforts.

The only active businesswoman among us was Mother

Superior. She attended to the utilities, the groceries, the orphanage, and all other expenses related to St. Joseph's, and somehow, despite minimum funds, managed to make ends meet. How she managed I'll never know, although her answer to a questioner was usually, "Budget, budget, budget, and *The Wall Street Journal*."

She was thankful for the fiscal relief provided by the telephone company, of course, but in the end her religious training was the winner. Along with the check covering the now standard monthly bill, she enclosed a note of gratitude for the utility's devout interest in the needy. Nothing happened. A month passed, another bill arrived, and again it was for the same twelve dollars and eighty cents. "Such beautiful people," said Mother Superior.

A week later, St. Joseph's welcomed a representative of the beautiful people. He explained that something mechanical had gone wrong in Accounting, and that was the reason the bill had been the same month after month after month. He laughed, and all the sisters present laughed, for he had told the story in a most amusing fashion. But all the fun went out of the story when he announced that we owed over nine hundred dollars. We didn't have to pay it immediately, of course, unless we wanted the vital phone service to continue. Mother Superior demanded the right to speak to somebody in authority. She, too, believed in going to the head of the class.

The next day, three gentlemen called upon her. One was an officer of the telephone company. The other two remained unidentified. They may have been bodyguards. They looked the type.

When the trio departed, our leader announced that we had ten days of grace. She had pleaded for a chance to pay off the debt on the installment plan, but without success. So she called a friendly lawyer for advice, and he promised to see what he could do, but he wasn't optimistic. He'd had previous experience with utilities.

It was then that she asked for my help. "Perhaps your friend the fire chief can do something?" she suggested. "But warn him that the official from the telephone company is a very stubborn man. Did you notice his jaw line? And he looked me right in the eyes. Business is business. Even if he'd been a Catholic, I don't think the Pope himself could have moved the man from his stand."

"By the way, what is his religion?" I asked.

"He's a Baptist."

So I paid another visit to my friend in the department of sanitation, Jersey City, New Jersey, and she talked to her boss, and that fine believer of clean speech promised to go into action.

Within a week, the telephone company recognized the error of its ways and agreed to settle the matter for three hundred dollars. St. Joseph's was able to raise that amount and enjoyed prompt service ever after. For many weeks thereafter, however, meat was scarce on the dinner table. The thirty-seven were content, for a little bit of history had been made: the first time a utility, a department of sanitation, Baptists, and Catholics agreed on anything.

I had been prepared to help all the needy in the world, but my first assignment as a junior nun was to help only two hundred: the girls and boys in our affiliated School and Home for the Blind. And my help for them was indirect.

St. Joseph's Home was a convent and printing plant. Two vintage presses churned out an amazing volume of printed material, including the quarterly *Orphans' Messenger and Advocate of the Blind* magazine—an important source of income. Unfortunately, the two presses did not work in harmony. One was usually resting and awaiting repairs while the other worked overtime. The thought that both would break down simultaneously never crossed our minds. Our faith in them was very strong. The jobs had to be done, the presses had to do the work, and one or the other always did. Some of the senior sisters treated the presses as if they were people. Sister Ruth, who could remember the start of the printing department, would enter the press room and shout over the din, "All right, boys! I prayed for you! Now let's meet this deadline!"

And the presses, or at least one of them, always did. The repair man, a pessimist of the first order, was forever assuring us that he could do nothing more to extend the longevities of our essential machines. For keeping them in working order, he considered himself a genius. He was unaware, of course, that we remembered him in our morning prayers.

I was informed during my third month at St. Joseph's that the magazine would become my first regular assignment.

"I've been wondering just how you'd fit in, Sister Vincent," the Superior told me, "for I knew He sent you here for a purpose. And then I remembered your Madison Avenue background. The magazine, of course!"

I considered her decision to be a wise one. I was the only refugee from Madison Avenue on the premises, I did have a flair for writing, and the magazine while it served its purpose well, could be developed even further.

Egotist that I was, I immediately had a dozen grand ideas, all designed to double the circulation and bring in that additional revenue needed for our work with the elderly blind and emotionally-retarded blind boys and girls.

With this in mind, I approached the editor-in-chief Sister Beatrice. "Sister, I would like to study some back issues of the magazine, I think our covers could stand improvement. They need more sell."

"True," agreed Sister Beatrice, "but professional art is costly. Now don't you worry about covers and editorial content. We must have circulation!"

As she talked on, I pieced little portions of her conversation together and learned, finally, the true nature of my mission. I was in complete charge of acquiring new subscriptions for the magazine! My title was Director of Public Relations. Gone were the dreams of competing with the *New Yorker* and *Look* magazines! (Little did I know, that years later, I would return as the editor. I wonder how I would feel if a young religious came up to me and said: "Sister, I think our covers need improvement).*"

"You're smiling, Sister Vincent. What are you thinking?"

I didn't tell her then, but I did later when we were good friends. A vision had come to me, and in it I was dressed in my long habit and knocking on a strange front door. A man opened the door and I said, "Pardon me, sir, but I'm soliciting subscriptions to the *Orphans' Messenger and Advocate for the Blind.* Cut rate. Would you help me work my way through St. Joseph's?"

Sister Beatrice wanted to run the vision as a cartoon in the magazine, but the Superior vetoed the idea. She was not against cartoons. Art was so costly.

So there I was, the new public relations director in full charge of obtaining new subscriptions by the dozens. While I was not a PR expert, I did know something about the field, all thanks to the Diet Hamburger Club of bygone years. I had been a member in good standing during my years along Madison Avenue. The club's members, all females, were all employed in communications, and three luncheon tables were reserved for us every business day at a favorite hamburger palace. The name of the club speaks for itself. The club's daily speakers were every member. We made many important decisions for the city, state, nation, and world. And we talked about our jobs, of course.

Now I remember two of the club's most popular definitions of public relations: (1) free advertising and (2) selling hot air before it cools off.

Neither definition would be of much help to me. There wasn't much chance of promoting the magazine in other media, and the publication was far too worthy to be classified as hot air. The sensible courses for me, I decided, was to circulate and vocalize. Go out and talk to people—not on an individual basis, but wholesale. Find groups.

The idea was approved by my superiors. "Be sure to explain the magazine's title, and that it is not printed in braille," was Sister Beatrice's advice. Mother Superior also had practical advice: "Speak to groups within walking distance. We don't have funds for transportation."

She also suggested that I start with school groups and told me not to underestimate the power of the young. According to her *Wall Street Journal*, American children wielded great influence in family circles. They forced their mothers to buy only certain brands of cereals and soaps and threatened to leave home if fathers didn't buy certain makes of cars. "American children, in effect, spend over forty billion dollars of their parents' money every year," said Mother Superior, lowering her voice to a confidential whisper. Then she winked and added, "Get a little piece of it for our worthy causes."

I spent a full week preparing my sales talk for the *Messenger and Advocate*. That meant writing and rewriting, memorizing, rehearsing before a mirror, trying out before little groups of sisters, listening to their comments, polishing, and then back to the mirror again. Then came a preview for Mother Superior.

"The speech is divine," she assured me, "but you are not a Bernhardt. Run through it again, but don't wave your arms, and take the emotion out of your voice."

Her criticism was just, but it didn't help my self-confidence. Nor did the sea of young faces I gazed upon when, in the next week, I faced my first school assembly. They were quiet and respectful and waiting for me to say something, and I was quite willing to say something, but the speech I'd so carefully rehearsed and memorized had somehow escaped my mind. So I began with, "When I was your age, I wanted to marry a cowboy."

The youngsters responded with laughter and then prolonged applause. It seemed ridiculous to them, I suppose, that a girl who wanted to marry a cowboy had somehow become a nun. They reacted as New Yorkers react to any remark about Brooklyn.

"Then I changed my mind and decided to become a jockey," I told them, and again the children laughed and applauded. They were there because they had to be there, but now I sensed they were happy about it and on my side. I made no attempt to recall what I'd planned to say to them, but I did make a mental note to remember my Brooklyn jokes for future youthful audiences.

It was a wonderful audience. I had been granted fifteen minutes but managed to get through twenty-five with the greatest of ease. It was an ad-lib speech all the way, a mixture of tales about blind youngsters of their age. Some of the stories were sad, some funny, and others devoted to children who had never seen a stove but could cook, or who had never seen dolls but could make them. And then, with a nod to the principal, whose gestures told me that I was running overtime, I would up with a plea for our little magazine and explained its purpose. "Take home one of the subscription blanks, and talk to your parents about it. I won't ask you to subscribe because the *Orphans' Messenger and Advocate of the Blind* is so expensive, and I wouldn't expect you to give up your allowances for six or seven months. The magazine costs a dollar a year."

That school, and the next few, were parochial ones, of course. I wanted to test my effectiveness on my own kind, or—to put it bluntly—ask for permission to speak from schools that weren't likely to turn me down. In the long run, that proved a needless fear. Only one public-school principal turned me down for "not wanting to set a precedent here," and later he changed his mind. I didn't know anyone on the board of education, but I did speak to my friend in the department of sanitation. The Baptists must have been strong in Jersey City.

"How did it go today, Sister Vincent?" asked Mother Superior during supper on the day of my first speaking assignment.

"Well, I took along two hundred subscription forms, and they all disappeared."

"Splendid" was all she said just then. But later, in her office, she had more to say: "I must confess that I phoned one of the teachers for her reaction. She told me that the children loved you. It seems that you're one of the funniest speakers they've ever heard. Now, I didn't think your speech was funny. Did you wave your arms?"

"I tried not to. I may have once or twice."

"I just don't understand. Have today's young people changed? Well, perhaps you'd better alter the speech here and there."

"I'll try," I promised. And I kept my promise. No two speeches were ever the same. When a story didn't achieve the desired effect, I dropped it and substituted something else the next time. A matter of trial, error, and correction. As the months slipped by, the girl who had wanted among other things to be a Broadway star started to realize a little part of that dream as a nun. I was becoming a star on the children's circuit in Jersey City, New Jersey. And no Broadway production ever boasted so many angels: the nine hundred sisters of the Order of St. Joseph who prayed daily for benefactors and offered 2,500 masses annually for the members who supported the blind children, the elderly blind, and the boys and girls from St. Joseph's Village.

Long before the year was over, I had exhausted the supply of public, private, and parochial schools in the Jersey City area. The saturation point had been reached. From then on, so far as young audiences were concerned, it was a matter of arranging bookings elsewhere and then trying to find transportation.

Finally, logistics became a real problem. Several times a week, the daily mail included invitations from school principals in relatively distant areas, such as the tip of Long Island. I attributed this to my growing fame, but the real credit belonged to the Social Six, the six sisters who spent part of each day writing letters of thanks to benefactors and friends of St. Joseph's Home. Many of those kind people lived quite a distance from Jersey City, and the enterprising sisters, happy to have something new to mention in their letters, were writing lines about Sister Vincent and portraying me as sort of a one-woman revivalist of vaudeville at the grade-school level.

I discovered this when I was assigned to the group and it became the Social Seven. So I was a nun with press agents. We were years ahead of the Vatican.

For all but one of the thirty-seven, the day began at 5:15 A.M. I don't know why the Brownie escaped the task—perhaps the responsibility was too great—but it was always a senior nun who awakened earlier and then made the rounds of the bedroom doors, knocking on each and saying sleepily, "*Benedicamus domino*" ("Let us bless the Lord"); and from the other side of the door, each of us would respond, even more sleepily, "*Deo gratias*," although it was a little rough to be grateful about anything that early in the morning.

Fifteen minutes later, we assembled for breakfast. Though we were adults and skipping breakfast was not a sin, it was a long time until noon and dinner, and snacks were not available. So all thirty-seven were usually at breakfast, where the mainstay was always an egg, always boiled, and never boiled long enough. The Superior believed in a "short-boiled" egg.

Somewhere along the line, perhaps in the pages of *The Christian Science Monitor*, she had learned that two minutes is long enough. If boiled longer, the egg's nutritional values seep through the shell and escape, and all the hen's work has been futile. The cook, of course, was anxious to please the Superior, so it was egg soup for the rest of us. The reason for eggs seven days a week was a friendly chicken farmer who sold them to us at wholesale and often forgot to send a bill. Unlike the telephone company, the bills that did arrive were for that month only and not retroactive. Short- or long-boiled, I now avoid a boiled egg wherever possible.

At six sharp we parted company and hurried off to our assigned duties. We gathered again at noon in the chapel for prayers, and then proceeded to the long table for dinner. I never did become accustomed to eating the day's big meal at midday, and doubt that I ever will. And I doubt that a nun's dinner will ever be served at a later hour. Our lives have changed and will continue to change in so many ways, but dinner must come at twelve twenty in our institutions. If we envy married women, it may be because they sit down to dinner at a more reasonable hour.

What the egg was to breakfast, the potato was to dinner. Large or small, they always managed to come to the table in a hard-boiled condition. The cook had learned his lesson well, and he wasn't about to lose any of the potato's valuable properties. Nor did he seem to know how to home-fry, scallop, mash, or bake the daily mainstay. Oddly, another vegetable, if present, was usually well cooked.

Meat was always present. Hamburger four or five times a week. It was served rare, and sometimes almost raw. Several of the nuns had been at St. Joseph's for over forty years. None liked rare meat, but they were healthy and thus living testimonials for the theory that the goodness resident in hamburger should not be cooked away. It was always fish on Friday, of course, although that late in the week it often tasted like more hamburger. Fried fish, and often fried to a crisp, as if the cook felt he had to overcook something for a change.

On days when hamburger and fish weren't present and the budget could stand the expense, we enjoyed chops or chicken. Fortunately, these were well cooked and instilled the hope in some of us that tomorrow might bring more-appetizing hamburger. It never happened, but the hope was always there.

Lemon Jell-O for dessert. I wondered aloud one day about that. Why was the flavor always the same? "The lemon is a citrus," my neighbor explained, "and like the carrot, it benefits the eyesight." The Superior nodded her agreement, so that was that.

An ample supply of potatoes always went back to the kitchen, and these reappeared when supper was served at six thirty. Sliced and diced, they became potato salad, the evening mainstay. We did our best to polish off the salad, for fear that the next night's salad would be only half new. Cold cuts and sardines, bread and butter, and occasional pickles and olives filled out the menu. It was supper at the novitiate all over again, except that we talked while dining and didn't listen in silence to a reader's rereading of a saint's life.

Mondays through Fridays, my work days were much the same: speaking assignments and/or helping to catch up on St. Joseph's correspondence. The Social Seven were always busy keeping abreast of the incoming mail from our friends throughout the country. Each letter was a labor of love, neat and phrased correctly, every word carefully chosen for its meaning. For the first time in my life, I found the dictionary a work of literary distinction and reliability. Each October, our pace slowed and we fell almost a month behind the incoming mail. The cause was World Series fever. We bet fantastic sums of imaginary dollars on every game. The Giants' sweep of Cleveland in 1954 cost me close to fifty thousand in hot air. Undaunted, I stayed with the Yankees all the way the next year and dropped another mint. I mention all this here to emphasize the fact that the religious life must have something in common with the great American game. Most of the nuns I've known have been baseball fans, although many have never attended a game. Team standings, batting averages, home-run leaders, earned run records, and stolen bases are a part of normal conversation in every convent in the land, in or out of season. My right hand is one of my most prized possessions. It once shook the right hand of Yogi Berra.

Saturdays were weary days, albeit special ones. The work week was over, but there was no rest for some of the weary minds. Along with a dozen other sisters—some of them college dropouts like myself—I climbed aboard the bus that would take us in the general direction of Seton Hall University in South Orange, New Jersey. The distance was twenty-odd miles, but the bus route was not a direct one, we changed buses three times en route, and we covered closer to seventy miles before reaching our campus destination. There were many small-town stops along the way, but few new passengers. It was a time-consuming journey for us and a money-losing one for the bus company. I pointed out these facts in a letter to the bus company, but it was even more immovable than the telephone company and did not take advantage of this nun's advice. A direct route would have saved both time and money.

Those who made the journey from St. Joseph's were in pursuit of college degrees. I majored in education and still think of a B.A. in terms of Saturdays. One hundred and eighty four of them, in my case. That's the way we found our higher education years ago, but today, thanks to grants, scholarships, and Pope John, nuns are full-time undergraduates on the campuses of many leading universities.

Sundays were our free days, or at least the afternoons were. Right after early Mass and breakfast, the basket brigades went into action. In teams of three and four, we stood outside the leading churches and appealed silently for funds. The duty was voluntary and the thirty-seven were never fully represented. Some of the sisters, of course, were elderly or suffering infirmities, and thus not up to the task. As I was a junior nun, it was expected of me. So I was one of the volunteers who didn't have to volunteer.

That Sunday income didn't amount to much, but we had a desperate need for every dollar we could find, and I was tempted to break the rule of silence. Whenever a Cadillac rolled to a stop and discharged its passengers, I wanted to rush up to those passengers and deliver an impassioned plea for monetary help. I was sure that they would empty their purses if I told them about the wonderful work St. Joseph's was doing. Some of the sisters thought the idea was a sound one. So I prepared a hundred-and-ten word selling message and found that I could deliver it in twenty seconds flat. The Superior vetoed the idea.

"I am surprised that you can't rattle off three hundred words in twenty seconds," she told me. "But, no! Definitely not! You would be delaying all churchgoers within sight. Save your words for speaking engagements."

But we were permitted to thank all those who contributed, and there was no rule to guide the manner of our thanks. Soon my team was saying "God bless you" to all who contributed, and "God love you" to those who passed us by. It was a fine distinction, but I was proud of it. It didn't take many Sundays for some Cadillac men and bejeweled women to decide they'd rather be blessed than loved.

Until then, the amount collected by each of the basket teams was about equal. There might be a variance of two or three dollars between the high and low teams, but seldom more. Now, Sunday after Sunday, my team was returning home with twenty-five or thirty dollars more than any of the others. The Superior suspected that we were doing something that we shouldn't be doing.

She did not ask any questions. Instead, and to our surprise, she accompanied us on a Sunday mission and observed my team in action.

"And bless all you clever ones, too," she said as we walked back to St. Joseph's. The very next Sunday, all our basket teams started using the same technique.

I didn't go along that day, and I never went again. Suddenly, I had become involved in a huge happening—a community dream that just had to become a reality.

The magazine didn't need me anymore. Annual subscriptions had zoomed to over ninety thousand, or just about all that the presses could bear. And the Social Seven could spare me, for there were new Brownies in the home.

Again, my new duty was in public relations, that cautious, religious misnomer for fund-raising. But this time I was expected to raise funds on the scale that they raise wheat in Kansas.

4

Last on the Menu

It was a week of surprises. It started in normal fashion, with two speaking engagements at schools on Monday and three on Tuesday. On Wednesday I spent the morning hours as one of the Social Seven, and then paid a long overdue visit to a local jewelry store.

Within a week I would be taking my final vows of poverty, chastity, and obedience. In honor of that day, St. Joseph's would present me with two gifts: a crucifix and a plain silver ring.

The visit to the jewelry store concerned the ring. Proper size had to be determined, and also the jeweler had to know just what to inscribe on the inner band. The inscription, a tradition in our community, would be a personal choice.

When I entered, the only other customer in the store was a gentleman. He was studying a tray of engagement rings. He looked up as I entered and motioned to the jeweler to wait on me. It was a tiny one-man store. Not the fanciest jewelry store in Jersey City, but the one selected by the community as the best of the lowest priced.

Once ring size had been decided, I told the jeweler about the words I wanted inscribed: *Sursum corda.*

"Spanish?" asked the jeweler.

"No, it's the Latin for 'Lift up your heart,' " said the gentleman customer. Then he turned to me and asked, "About ready to take your final vows?"

"I am."

"Then lift up your head and start thinking! What's wrong with you? Don't you believe in being normal?"

I had no chance to reply. He was off and running, waving an index finger in my face, banging his fist on a counter, and loosing a tirade of accusations—none of them admirable. I had heard them all before, but never presented with so much conviction and enthusiasm. He was sure that a woman's sole reason for being is to marry and bear children. I don't know whom he was buying the engagement ring for, but if they ever married, then that woman had a husband who would never stray from wedlock.

His barrage of words lasted three or four minutes and concluded with, "And I'd tell you the same things if I were a

Catholic instead of a Lutheran!" With that he marched out of the store.

The Superior was all smiles when I returned to the home. "The jeweler just phoned," she told me. "You were there at just the right time. The Lutheran gentleman you met there returned after you left and insisted on paying for your ring. You should write a note of thanks to him.* Well, Sister Vincent, first the Baptists, now the Lutherans. Who next?"

The other major surprise of the week took place on Friday evening after supper. It started with this casual question from the Superior: "How up-to-date are you on the village?"

"Not very," I told her. "I know that ground has been broken and that things have been moving along."

"Have you any idea of what this will cost us by the time it's completed?"

I did not. I had never hired a carpenter, never purchased lumber or brick, and never bought a chair. I just didn't know costs, and wasn't even qualified to give a silly estimate. So I told her so.

"More than five million dollars," Mother Superior informed me. "It seemed exorbitant to me, but that's what the experts tell us. Think of it! Five million dollars! Sometimes I wonder where we'll find it. Isn't it too bad that faith doesn't have a cash value? If we could only mortgage our faith!"

The village we were discussing was the dream I mentioned before. It had a formal name—St. Joseph's Village for De-

---

* I would have, but the jeweler would not reveal the gentleman's name. I never saw my benefactor again, but if our paths ever do cross, I'll thank him first and then tell him that now we sing Martin Luther's hymns during Holy Communion.

pendent Children—and it was in the process of construction on fifty-seven acres in Rockleigh, New Jersey. Plenty of space and plenty of fresh air, bounded on one side by a golf course and on the other by an industrial park.

Plans for the dream had started with the fire in Englewood Cliffs, the one that had destroyed our boys' orphanage when I was a senior novice at St. Michael's. It was one of three orphanages* run by my order. The two others, both for girls, were located in North Bergen and at our home in Jersey City. The dream, when it became a reality, would be all three orphanages under one roof. One big family.

It was a practical dream in terms of economy, supervision, and growth. And it had many human side benefits, such as bringing together the separated children of one family.

When it became a reality, the village would be a model of its kind. The children would live in separate cottages, each with a capacity of twenty-four, and all twenty-four in the same age range. Every cottage would come equipped with a housemother (a sister) and a lay houseparent (female). It would be the same for the boys, except for the lay houseparent. A man, of course. And all cottages would boast a kitchen, laundry room, individual closets, garden, and (sometimes) pets. Only one of the cottages would be coeducational; it would be for the tiniest tots. Overall, a community of family-style cottages, and a far cry from the usual orphanage.

There would be other buildings, of course: living quarters for the sisters, administration, dining rooms, classrooms, auditorium, and storage. Seventeen in all.

* While we think of the children as orphans, few are—in the strict sense of the word. Most of the youngsters are from broken, unhappy, or impoverished homes. They range in age from four to fifteen years.

But all of it was years and five million dollars away.

"In this situation, we could use a singing nun," said the Superior.

I didn't know what she was talking about, but I nodded in agreement, anyway. That was years before the advent of the famous Belgian nun, all those recordings, and the Debbie Reynolds film.

"Fortunately, we do have a talking nun," she continued, smiling and then winking at me. "We've been discussing the idea for weeks, and we've reached a unanimous conclusion. You are relieved of your other duties and will begin at once."

I nodded, but I didn't say anything. Again, I didn't know what she was talking about.

"Any questions, Sister Vincent?"

"Just one comes to mind," I said. "Just what am I starting on at once?"

"Fun-raising, of course," she replied.

"Fun-raising?" I wondered if Pope John had decreed something I hadn't heard about. Was pure fun a part of renewal? "Fun-raising?" I asked, as all sorts of idiotic thoughts flashed through my brain.

"We must find that five million dollars somewhere. If not through *fund*-raising," said Mother Superior, emphasizing the word this time, "then where else?"

The racetrack appealed to me. I could have fun there raising funds if St. Joseph's would stake me to a couple of thousand.

It was just a thought. I didn't express it.

"Do you think you can raise three or four million, Sister Vincent?"

"Alone?"

"Not really. You shall have the very best assistance."

I was relieved to hear that. Fund-raising on a big scale means organization, and organization means people. "For a start," I said, "I'll need at least five or six sisters who are experienced in working with committees."

"Oh, we can't spare any of the sisters for this project of yours," the Superior explained. "When I spoke of the very best assistance, I was speaking of Him, of course."

She was right. Who could ask for more?"

It was nice to know that He was on my team. Finding two or three million would be a cinch.

But it didn't work out that way, and for a long time I wondered if I'd ever reach the hundred-thousand-dollar mark.

I loved to talk and was willing to do so around the clock. But my reputation as a speaker, such as it was, was on the youth circuit. Now I had to find adult audiences, for that's where the important money was.

And adult audiences were not easy to find. I suppose it's an American tradition, but guest speakers are mostly drawn from the male ranks. That's one good reason why there are so few women in politics. Who wants to listen to a woman? Ever hear of one on the banquet circuit? And who wants to listen to a woman if she's a nun? What can a nun contribute to a gala event?

So bookings were rough to come by at the start. Most of the early invitations were arranged by friends, and for months I found myself addressing female-only audiences. Mother-and-daughter dinners, garden-club luncheons, League of

Women Voters and secretarial club meetings, became my specialties, but I preferred the luncheons and dinners. There's some sort of relationship between food and tolerance. Once her appetite is satisfied, a woman makes a better listener.

I wasn't at all nervous facing adult audiences, but the ladies were more difficult to warm up than their children. They were always willing to smile, but there were times when they just wouldn't laugh. Captive audiences, but not very responsive, and I began to think that I could read the private thoughts of many of my happily married listeners: "Just one more appeal for money, and there will be ten more appeals in my mail today. Baby, am I happy that I married Harry and didn't wait for Wilbur, or I might be standing here as a sister and holding out my hand for money. What a life!"

"Thank you, Madam Chairman. I would like to begin by assuring all of you that I am not a mind reader," I said one day. "Still, it would be a miracle and quite unlike human nature if a few of you here today weren't thinking at this very moment about my private life. Those few are wondering why I decided to devote myself to God's service and why I never married. Well, ladies, I'm going to make a confession. I had my chances, and I blew every one of them!" The ladies gasped, laughed, and applauded. They were on my side. I reached new speaking heights that day and have used the same opening remarks many times since.

To my surprise, it always came as news to the ladies when I told of the work done by the sisters at our orphanages. That we were the teachers in the classrooms was understandable, but the majority of my listeners were unaware that we also did all the cooking, nursing, washing, mending, sewing, decorating, and general housekeeping. The nun in an orphanage, in addition to being a sort of wholesale mother, makes the average suburban housewife look like a minor leaguer.

The fact that not all our orphans were of the Catholic faith also came as news. I think that helped the dream village as much as the mention that brothers and sisters would be reunited in one orphanage. But the little stories that had amused or saddened the schoolchildren didn't go over well with the ladies. Perhaps they were thinking of cuter stories about their own youngsters.

Before two many months went by, I was averaging about ten speeches a week, and invitations were coming in from distant points. Still, I was disappointed, for the funds traceable to my talks were anything but impressive. Our devoted *Wall Street Journal* reader kept assuring me that I was on the right track with such encouraging remarks as "Women control the purse strings of America" and "Women have more checking accounts than men," but I was proof of neither.

And then, in a small way, I became living proof. A letter arrived from a complete stranger. Well, a stranger to all of us at St. Joseph's, but not unknown to us, for she was often in the press. She had social position, wealth, and a great reputation as a humanitarian. "A friend told me about a talk given by your Sister Vincent in Newark some weeks ago," she wrote. "For years I have been interested in homeless dogs, cats, and other pets. I do hope the children in your new orphanage will be permitted to have pets. They are so important to the young. Please accept this little check."

The little check was in five figures. It was repeated by the donor over the next several years. None of us ever met her, and she's gone now. The children in our village do have pets.

I've met a great many self-appointed humanitarians since

then and told them that story, and most were able to guess her identity. And almost all missed the moral. They didn't reach for their checkbooks, not even those wearing mink or sable. Sometimes it doesn't pay to be subtle.

The little check gave me my first big lift. The next came at a supper held by the ladies of a Dutch Reformed Church. I had delivered my speech and was saying my good-byes when an elderly lady approached, took my hands in hers, and said, "Sister, I didn't realize until tonight that a nun is a real human being."

I smiled and nodded my thanks. For once, I was at a loss for words. But while I didn't know what to reply, I knew that at last—at long last—I was beginning to reach the adult public.

"Did she seem like a rational person?" asked the Superior.

"Very," I assured her.

"Have you ever thought of yourself as anything but a human being? Since you became a nun, I mean."

"No."

"Nor have I. But I suppose most lay people do regard us as a bit odd. The good ones consider themselves devoted to His service, but they don't take vows or dress in ancient manner or sacrifice certain pleasures. An aura of mystique surrounds us, wouldn't you say? We're appreciated, but not fully understood. Well, Sister Vincent, you've achieved a breakthrough! And there is an explanation. Your face. The map of Ireland is on your face, so you must be a human being."

I had no speaking engagements lined up for several days, so there was plenty of time for deep thinking. At the rate I was going, I could talk every day for the next two hundred years and still fall short of three million dollars. Would the women I had talked to ever twist their husbands' arms and high-pressure them into permitting me to address male audiences? It hadn't happened, and there was no sign that it ever would. My own father wouldn't have invited me to his club, but he would have advised me to go to the head of the class.

So I did. In two days' time, I wrote over fifty letters to leading professional and business men in the area, outlining the plans for the village, the need for funds, my experiences until then, and asking for advice. You can be sure that the Baptist head of the department of sanitation was on the list. I didn't bother to find out about the religions of the other gentlemen. My Assistant wouldn't worry about that.

If there was a touch of genius in the letter, it was in the asking for advice. The thirty-two gentlemen who responded had plenty of advice, and all of it boiled down to two words: Think Big.

The first big thinking resulted in the formation of an all-male advisory board for St. Joseph's Village. And from that board's first meeting came plans for something we called The Affair, a dinner-dance at one hundred dollars a plate! "If we can do it for politicians, we can certainly do it for dependent children," a dentist assured me. He knew what he was talking about and has been my personal dentist ever since.

A lawyer suggested *The Journal*, really the program for the dinner-dance. I considered it an unnecessary expense until he explained the profit derived from advertising space. The Friends of St. Joseph's Village sponsored *The Journal*, our presses printed it, it was no hardship soliciting ads, and the profit was enormous.

Never underestimate male reasoning. It may be true that the women of America control the purse strings, but surely it's the men who fill the purse. I don't know what we'd have done without The Affair and *The Journal*. They were great successes from every viewpoint, the fiscal in particular, and have become firmly established as annual events. They started during the second Eisenhower Administration, and the price of admission remains at one hundred dollars per plate. So we've held the line on the high cost of living. No sense in changing anything that's realized over a million dollars in a dozen years.

THINK BIG! screamed the sign. It was a gift from a lay friend. The letters were red and about a foot high. I hung it on the wall facing my desk. When I went to my room before supper, I found the door covered with slightly smaller but similarly worded signs. Twenty more were tacked on the walls of my room. The print shop pranksters had worked overtime.

Despite such encouragement, none of my big thinking produced—or ever would produce—a million dollars at one crack. Nor did my thoughts produce the male audiences I was so anxious to address. The advisory board worked overtime giving advice on the things even nuns must know about a building program—mortgages, interest, insurance, contracts—but none of the board members seemed interested in arranging bookings for the talking nun.

So I went to another head of the class. I wrote a letter to Washington. Not to the President, but to a senator from New Jersey who was running for reelection. I didn't know him, but he was aware of St. Joseph's. Years before when he'd won his first election, his wife had been one of our volunteer workers.

It was a short, honest letter. I asked for his help in finding speaking engagements in the male world, explained our great need for funds, and reminded him that all nine hundred sisters were good citizens and regular voters. I also wrote a separate letter to his wife, thanking her for past favors and advising that I was writing to her husband.

I did not hear directly from either of them, but the good senator was not a man to overlook nine hundred votes. Two weeks later, thanks to his influence, I was the guest speaker at my first all-male event: the annual breakfast for the blue-collar workers of one of the nation's leading breweries. It wasn't Congress, but it was a start.

The breakfast was held in Manhattan, and the beer company sent a limousine to Jersey City to pick me up. On other days, the chauffeur drove a beer truck. He had borrowed the car from his brother, an undertaker, and he drove it as if his brother needed new business. The journey started at seven in the morning, and one of history's deepest fogs didn't stop us from reaching Manhattan in world's record time. The friendly truck driver kept assuring me that he could see, but I didn't know we'd crossed the George Washington Bridge until he told me. It was a ride I'll never forget. There were moments when I wondered if my Assistant had forgotten me.

"Well, here we are," said the driver, "and do you know what I've been thinking while we talked?"

I hadn't said a word. He'd been doing all the talking, and I'd learned many things: his life story, the joys of driving a beer truck, the trouble with French women, how to discern an honest wrestler, what was wrong with the man in the White House, and that he—a twenty-year veteran with his company —preferred two other brands of beer. Now he told me what he had been thinking about:

"You and me are compatible because we're in the same business, sort of. I mean, ain't we both serving mankind? You with help, me with beer."

I didn't laugh. He said it seriously. I suppose it's the only reason I remember it. The ride had shattered me, and now his philosophy depressed me. What was I walking into? Was the Senator friend or enemy?

Breakfast was served to four hundred men and one woman. I sat at the head table with a dozen beer-company executives. Charming men, and we got along famously until the waiter asked, "Coffee or beer?" I didn't want to insult my hosts, so I ordered beer. All my hosts ordered coffee. Misguided ethos on my part. That one word of courtesy from me had put the reputations of a million nuns in jeopardy. Only the waiter acted as if he hadn't heard me. The wise man brought coffee to my place.

The dinner that was misnamed breakfast was accompanied by spirited music from a German band. Then as the hall filled with cigar smoke, there was a series of short pep talks, the awarding of twenty-five-year pins, and finally—last on the menu—the guest of honor, Sister Vincent.

At long last, and at an unlikely hour, I was on my feet and about to address an audience of adult males. "Well, here's the pitch!" were the words I used for an opener, borrowing them from the undertaker's brother. He'd used them at least a hundred times earlier that morning. This brought the laugh I needed to break the ice. "You have a fine product, and I know what I'm talking about. Back in the days when it was possible to be independent, my father owned a grocery store. Your brand was his best seller and his personal favorite. So I'm on your side. Now, we've just heard about your record sales to taverns, hotels, and retail outlets. I didn't hear anything about convents. I can't help you there, and I don't know of anyone who can. But if prayers will help in other areas, you can count on me. In return, I want you to come over to my side. Forget about religion, forget that I'm a nun, and give me three minutes to tell you about a certain village."

They gave me twenty minutes, contributed over two thousand dollars, and I haven't turned down a breakfast invitation from gentlemen since. And while I'm against billboards in general, somehow that beer company's highway signs always seem to enhance the scenery.

A couple of weeks later, on a narrow highway in Pennsylvania, a huge truck almost ran me off the road. It then stopped in front of me, blocking the way and causing me to stop. The driver jumped from his cab, walked to my car, looked at me, nodded, and said, "I thought it was you, Sister Vincent. Say, you were just great at our breakfast! So I was wondering, would you be interested in talking to my American Legion post in Brooklyn?"

I was, and I did. And suddenly, the floodgates opened. Invitations to address all sorts of male groups poured in. One senator and one driver of a beer truck got the ball rolling, and it has been rolling ever since. Elks, Rotarians, Lions, Masons, Veterans of Foreign Wars, colleges, a variety of labor unions, press clubs, civic organizations, church groups of all denominations, manufacturers, insurance companies, granges, Audubon societies, conservationists, highway departments, hospitals, educators, state and federal agencies, theater and literary clubs, dairymen, industrialists, and sports fans.

And that's not a complete list. Over a period of ten years, I've delivered billions of spoken words in thousands of speeches at breakfasts, luncheons, dinners, dances, conventions, and just plain meetings. Audience sizes have varied from about fifty listeners to over forty thousand, from club room to football stadium. The setting has usually been a hotel ballroom or a convention hall or a church basement or the dining room of a country club, but sometimes I've made my plea for the village in the great outdoors—frequently at picnics, a score of times at clambakes, and once in an amphitheater. We don't have a computer at St. Joseph's, but the keeper of the records informed me in 1961 that my oratorical efforts had brought in over two million dollars. She also presented me with a small supply of calling cards from my prankster friends in the print shop. It carried this slogan in bold italics: *Have Gift of Gab, Will Travel.* With a forged autograph of Charles Chaplin attached, they brought five dollars apiece at a dinner-dance the following night. The children's food bill at the village now runs better than nine thousand a month, and every little dollar counts. Mr. Chaplin knows about child upkeep. We didn't think he'd mind.

In the beginning, a dozen years ago, I worried about being cast in the role of last on the menu. No matter how many speakers were present, I was always the last to be presented. It seemed to me that the master of ceremonies was using me as a hint that the end was near and that soon everyone could go home and be happy. Today, being last doesn't concern me. I think my Assistant planned it that way, for the results have been bountiful.

Most of my speaking engagements have been in the East. Even in this jet age, distance remains a problem, for public speaking is just one of my duties as a nun. Still, nuns do enjoy vacation time, and I've been able to combine travel with speeches in far-off states: Illinois, Ohio, Texas, Colorado, Wisconsin, and California.

It hasn't happened yet, but I still hope to address a group of ranchers. I suppose that yen dates back to my girlhood dream of marrying a cowboy, because a cowboy meant horses. I'll never realize that girlish dream, of course, but I haven't forgotten the horses. I didn't lose my love for those noble beasts, and counted that year unfulfilled when I wasn't able to spend at least a few hours at the National Horse Show in Manhattan.

The village was well along and some of the cottages were occupied when a group of the sisters decided that the vast expanse of still-vacant acreage should be put to some practical use. Raising crops or sheep or cattle were practical thoughts, but there wasn't a farmer's daughter among us, nor did we have the ready cash for equipment or livestock. An annual outdoor event of some kind seemed to be the best idea. A bazaar or country fair or a circus. I volunteered the thought that a horse show might prove profitable. The open land was level, and in my innocence I thought that the only expense would be the renting of bleachers. The suggestion was greeted with a fine lack of enthusiasm. The sisters started discussing other ideas. In the end, it was decided that everyone would do more thinking. "Think big!" I told them.

Several days later, a visiting priest asked, "How are the plans for the show coming along?"

"What show?" was my reply. We had several on the schedule: a magic show for the children; an art show featuring oils, water colors, and sculptures created by St. Joseph's nuns; and a Night of Music starring our Choral Sisters and guest celebrities. Only the first would represent a fiscal loss: the fee for the magician.

"The horse show," said the good man. "I suppose all the sisters will ride sidesaddle?"

I did a little checking. Sure enough, the decision to stage a horse show had been made, but none of the sisters had told me. "When do you plan to hold it? Next month?" one of them asked. The snow was two feet deep at the time.

Take it from me, anyone in a great hurry to stage a horse show might as well forget about it. For the next seventeen months, I spent from minutes to hours every day working on our horse show. First, we had to qualify as responsible sponsors. Then, since the horse-show circuit is a busy one, we had to await the assignment of an open date. Once that date had been secured, we plunged into advance publicity and mailings, plus a large-scale hunt for appropriate trophies. We arranged for bleachers, food concessions, tents, road-direction signs, police, ribbons, certificates, jumps, judges, veterinarians, public-address system, and all the incidental equipment needed at a horse show.

"Renting bleachers will be the only expense," became a favorite phrase among the sisters. Long before the day of our first horse show, it was apparent that I'd underestimated the overhead by about eight thousand dollars.

I wasn't worried. The novelty of a horse show run by nuns had appealed to the horse fancy, and entries were coming in from all over the country. Most of the riders would be in the East for the other shows on the circuit, anyway. So I knew we'd have the horses, and if we could fill the bleachers, our profit would amount to a few thousand dollars. Still, that didn't seem enough for seventeen months of planning. I ordered more bleachers.

None of us worried about the weather. We took it for granted that it would be a fair and sunny day, and it was. Also, it was an SRO (Standing Room Only) day, and my one regret was that I hadn't ordered more bleachers. I just hadn't been thinking big enough, but I corrected that oversight the next year.

The first annual Sisters of St. Joseph's Horse Show was a thirty-thousand-dollar success. The second did even better, and the third topped the second.

Rain fell on the day before the fourth annual horse show. Nine hundred sisters and three hundred children prayed for the rain to stop. It dwindled to a light sprinkle just after midnight, and I fell asleep thinking that the last of the Jewish holidays was just beginning—always a sunny day for as far back as I could recall—and now we had two strong faiths going for us. Surely the sun would come.

But it didn't. I awoke to pouring rain, and it seemed to increase in intensity all during the hours of the horse show. The grounds were a sea of mud. The bleachers were almost empty. Our food concessions did very little business. Only the horses were happy.

Our loss for the day was over five thousand dollars. For the next three weeks, frankfurther was the meat in our diets. We lost our taste for frankfurters and horse shows.

And what about all those prayers? I guess we didn't start early enough, for they were heard. We're sure of that. The rain stopped and the setting sun broke through the clouds as the last horse vans pulled away from the grounds.

That other girlhood dream of mine—the one about becoming a Broadway star—has never been realized, either. But in a way, I've come close.

The Astor Hotel doesn't stand on Broadway anymore, but while it was still there we held the first of a series of annual all-star benefit shows in the main ballroom. Weather wasn't a factor, so they were safer bets than the horse shows. The overhead was fixed: ballroom rental and orchestra. All of the acts, including the big stars, performed gratis. The only amateurs were our Choral Sisters. Unfortunately, we didn't have the talent for a Choral Orchestra.

Tickets were twenty dollars a head, and for guests who hated to go home early, dancing into the wee hours followed the entertainment. At the first show, I made my almost-Broadway debut in the company of such stars as Horace Mc-Mann, Connie Boswell, Carmel Quinn, and James Brown. I had rehearsed my one line: "Ladies and gentlemen, thank you for coming, and please stay for dancing after the show." An instant ad lib came to mind, so I added it: "And by the way, I will be up in Suite 409."

The instant ad lib brought down the house. I walked off-stage to the accompaniment of laughter, applause, and shouts of "Encore, Encore." The innocent invitation to my two-room headquarters suite, where I was spending the night (courtesy of the hotel), would haunt me for many months. During question-and-answer periods followed my talks, somebody in the audience was bound to stand and ask, "And how are things in 409, Sister Vincent?"

Eight months later and a hundred miles from Manhattan, a priest at a Communion breakfast turned to me and asked, "And how did things go in 409, Sister Vincent?"

"Who told you about that?" I wanted to know.

"The mayor. He and his wife were there that night. Ever since, people around here have been playing 409 and turning their winnings over to the parish." And as I was leaving he asked, "By the way, sister, did anyone ever win that car?"

"A man from the Bronx. I think he was a plumber."

"Do you remember the lucky number?"

I did, because it was an easy one to remember: 3366.

"I'll pass the number along," the priest promised. "I think 409 has run out its string. Winnings have been light of late."

The car raffle had produced about a third of the twenty-five-thousand-dollar profit we'd realized from the first show and dance at the Astor. We'd been selling tickets for weeks. People who thought the show tickets were priced too high— ever after the income-tax-deduction advantage had been explained—were almost sure to buy a couple of one-dollar raffle tickets. Anything to get rid of us, I suppose.

A sister we had dubbed Sister Caution was in charge of the raffle. She had made arrangements through lay friends to buy the new car at dealer's price, which meant a substantial saving. But she refused to actually buy the car until a sufficient number of tickets had been sold to cover the cost. Then, when the money was in hand, she still refused to buy. It was her belief that the winner might not want a new car. "You never know," she assured us. "Some people hate cars." She was prepared to thank such an unusual winner, not substitute cash for the car, and accept praise for having run a perfect raffle.

Sister Caution was dedicated to selling those raffle, tickets.

All during the dancing at the Astor, she and her team of selling agents—nuns and volunteer lay friends—buttonholed the dancers and sold hundreds of additional tickets. They sold right down to the deadline, one o'clock in the morning. Then, just as advertised, the big barrel was placed on the stage, trumpets blared, and Sister Caution marched into the spotlight. The big moment for the drawing!

"Ladies and gentlemen," announced Sister Caution, "I regret telling you that I forgot to bring all the stubs from tickets sold prior to tonight. They are in my room at St. Joseph's Home, 81 York Street, Jersey City, New Jersey, third floor, front. So we can't hold the drawing at this time. By the way, we still have several hundred tickets available."

On a rainy day in the next week, I accompanied Sister Caution as she drove a borrowed pickup truck over the Hudson and into Manhattan and the Astor. There the barrel was loaded on the truck. We drove from there to a friend's home in Sparkhill, New York, unloaded the barrel, added the missing stubs to its contents, and held the drawing for the new car. To keep within the rules of the raffle commission, the drawing had to be held in New York State.

"Find me a disinterested, honest person to draw the lucky number," requested Sister Caution as she mixed the stubs with both hands and both arms.

So I walked up the street to a bus stop, found an honest-looking man, and asked him if he'd like to perform the task. He was not only disinterested, but confessed that he was inexperienced in the lottery business. But he didn't know how to turn down a nun. On the walk back to the house, I learned that he was a plumber and an atheist.

The gentleman stuck his hand in the barrel, withdrew lucky

stub 3366, and hurried off to meet his bus. Sister Caution then telephoned the winner in the Bronx. "You are under no obligation to accept the car," she told him, but he said he would accept it, anyway, and that his favorite automotive color was red in the tone of medium rare. He volunteered the information that he was a plumber by trade and a Methodist on Sundays. So the plumbers had something going for them, but not the atheists.

On our trip to Manhattan and then Sparkhill, Sister Caution had driven the truck as if she'd never driven one before, which was precisely the case. But on the homeward journey to Jersey City that night, she drove with the reckless abandon of an expert, and I kept my eyes closed much of the time. It had not been the perfect raffle after all, for the winner wanted his loot. She would have to buy the car and see that it was delivered. "Do you think the Lord will understand if I buy a purple one?" she asked at one point. "I've worked so hard, and it will give me a little personal satisfaction."

Well, either He wasn't listening or He did understand, for she did indulge in her little satisfaction and nothing ever happened. To this day, she holds nothing against plumbers or Methodists, but she never visits the Bronx.

Or was He listening? When we reached home that evening, a committee of the Friends of St. Joseph's Village was in session. The chairman congratulated Sister Caution for the fiscal success of the car raffle and then explained that the committee had decided to hold several raffles each year, tying in each raffle with a scheduled fund-raising event. "You're our raffle expert, so you'll be in complete charge of that end," the chairman advised her. "Securing the prizes, printing the tickets, organizing the selling campaigns, holding the drawing, and all the other little details."

Until her recent transfer, Sister Caution was an outstanding success. She developed the securing of prizes into a fine art, and sometimes managed to find them at no cost to us. Those were the ones that she considered perfect raffles. And a few years ago, she achieved the ultimate: the ideal perfect raffle. The prize was a pony, and the winner was a bachelor who lived in a small apartment, didn't like ponies, and thought the entire thing was a gag. The whole raffle was news to him. Apparently, a friend had bought the winning ticket in his name. He told Sister Caution to keep the pony or give it to somebody else. His refusal didn't cause any hardship. Sister Caution had a certain pony in mind, but she hadn't purchased it.

The Friends of St. Joseph's Village, by the way, deserve far more than passing comment. I don't know where the village would be without them. They are all members of the lay community, men and women who volunteer their time and skills in the helping-hands department. Some devote a few hours a week, others several days a week, to the specific areas of work that interest them. Help is always needed and accepted gratefully in such facets of village life as teaching, sewing, transportation, supervision of children's trips to museums or historic sites or beaches, nursing, decorating, correspondence, mailings, gardening, and general repair. Then there's the work of the ever-abundant committees and guilds calling for long planning and longer follow-through. They specialize in programs designed for specific purposes: to put more books in the library, to find new clothes for the children, to provide toys and playground equipment, to buy instruments for the juvenile band, and always, always, to dream up new, appealing ways to raise funds that will help reduce the mortgage and meet overhead, on one hand, and help building expansion, on the other, so that we can retain what we have while we increase the number of children under our care.

I talk too much. I know that. Nobody has to tell me. Still, I've been a sister now for eighteen years, and lightning hasn't touched me. I figure Somebody Up There approves.

But you shouldn't push your luck forever. Thus, on the occasion of my seventeenth anniversary as a sister, I considered it high time for me to concentrate in a single direction. I knew I would be a nun for the rest of my life. If all the years to come could be concentrated in one area, then I'd be content and might even become an expert.

My superiors were not surprised to hear of my desire. They approved the idea, after first pointing out that other sisters of St. Joseph's had been doing just that for a long, long time. I hadn't noticed.

"And what do you think that you do best, Sister Vincent?"

I almost told them. Ever since Pope John, the thing I'd been doing best, by word and deed, was pushing the spirit of renewal for all it was worth. I hate hats, but I'm as fashion conscious as the next woman. I'm as eager to be a part of the scene as the next person. I want to belong in all ways. In short, I want to be as real as can be. But I couldn't tell them that. They were older, set in their ways, changing over to the new times but not in haste.

"I'm sure you can judge that better than myself," I said.

"We'll think about it," I was advised. "For the present, just continue."

I did.

And the next time we met, it was as if we'd had no previous meeting. They asked me for my reports, then excused me. So far as I know, they're still thinking about my desire.

Meanwhile, in the spirit of renewal and in the hope that I will not reach old age before my time, I've been conserving my energies. While I still talk too much, I don't talk as much as before. Not in public, anyway. A few years ago, for example, I was making better than twenty speeches a week. The current average is seventeen weekly bookings, and I intend to cut that down. The trouble is where to start. Even though the grapefruit is usually tired, I don't want to eliminate Communion breakfasts. They've been very productive, and early-morning speaking sort of sweeps the cobwebs from my mind.

At luncheons and dinners, the food is fine and the audiences very attentive. Still, the wisest move may be to cut down on those dinner engagements. I've been advised against night driving, especially where a long trip is involved. I hate to drive alone at night and usually take along another sister or a lay friend, and they are the ones who have been advising me not to drive at night. It is their unanimous opinion that while traffic is not necessarily more dangerous at night, I am.

For nine years, I served as Sister Public Relations for the village. While the duty was mostly a matter of public speaking, all sorts of assignments come under the general heading of public relations, from finding talent to entertain the children to running guided tours of the village. And once the village became a reality, somebody decided that I wasn't busy enough and then I started wearing two hats, the second that of Sister Moderator. This meant involvement with all the volunteer individuals and groups who came under the big umbrella of the Friends of St. Joseph's Village.

Now I was truly on the run. There weren't enough hours in the day. I was aware of that after my first week, but it took two years of subtle hints before my superiors became aware. Finally a junior sister was appointed as my assistant, and we started moderating full blast. And I was so happy. After too many years, I had reached executive level.

We sat in on all committee meetings, helped organize and promote events that ran the gamut from fashion luncheons to cake sales, and gave guidance when asked and when we felt qualified. Overall, we were the representatives of all the other sisters and did our best to keep things moving smoothly and effectively. In the beginning, I think I functioned moderately well as a moderator. But then the Friends grew, committees became abundant, and activities multiplied. No one was able to tell me how to be in three places at the same time. I requested more assistance.

It came in the form of a tape recorder. This was a help, but not much. It, too, could be in only one place at a time, and was of no help at all when it came to the innumerable phone calls. Incoming phone calls of an unclassified nature fell within the jurisdiction of the moderator, and nine calls out of ten were considered to be unclassified by the sister who was on answering duty.

I, of course, did not sit by the telephone. My hours at the village were filled mostly by moderating and minor public-relationing, so I was paged over the public-address system: "Phone call for 62." Every sister had a number, and mine was

62. I also responded to "Phone call for 409"; it depended on which sister was monitoring the system—some were wittier than others.

The architect of our administration buildings must have been a specialist in long corridors. I think he planned the corridors first, then added the rooms and the roofs. So I was usually a long way from the telephone when my number was called. When I heard the number, I dropped what I was doing, hopped aboard my trusty yellow scooter, and scooted off for the phone. There were no major accidents. Those who noted my coming stepped aside and hugged the wall.

Some of the phone calls were easy to answer: "Can you use me for three hours on Wednesday mornings?" or "Would you like some juvenile science books for the library?" or "I have four seats to a Broadway show on Saturday night. Would the sisters like them?"

Some were pathetic: "My wife left me. Can I bring my kids over today and leave them with you?" or the reverse: "Listen, what do I have to do to get my kid back? Kidnap her? Listen, Harry is going to get a job and I'm not drinking so much. So what do you say?"

And every so often there was a strange call, such as "How would you like a cow?" My answer to that one was in the negative, but I congratulated the hopeful donor for his deep, practical thinking. Our children consumed over three hundred quarts of milk a day, and I often thought that we could have saved money by operating our own small dairy farm. All that spare acreage. I never suggested it, however, for I knew who would be moderating the cows. And one thing would lead to another. Chickens next, then beef cattle. Milk, eggs, and meat are the basics we still serve in the thousand meals a day. And none of the sisters, as I mentioned, were raised on farms.

Sister Assistant Moderator was a great help in that moderating business. Together, we were able to cover five or six committee meetings in one afternoon. My scooter helped me, but she—being much younger—walked. But as the moderating business continued to expand, she felt the need of an assistant. I agreed.

Away from public relations and moderating, I spent my free time with the children, helping wherever needed. There were always some who wanted to go home, although they had no home to go to. And others who had real or imaginary problems, and still others who needed help with their studies. But the free time was hard to find.

About a year after I had sent a request through channels for an assistant to assist Sister Assistant Moderator, the request was granted. Another tape recorder.

A day later, my assistant took over as Sister Moderator. I wished her luck and gave her my yellow scooter. I wouldn't need it where I was going.

I was right back where I'd started as a junior professed nun in Jersey City. Back in the convent as Sister Editor of the *Orphans' Messenger and Advocate of the Blind.* I'd been away from the quarterly for over nine years, and the new assignment pleased me. It meant concentrating my efforts in one direction, or almost. I still hold to that average of seventeen speeches a week, although these days the subject is usually renewal, and the fees go to our program for the blind.

So now I'm Sister Editor and Sister Speaker, and I'm still on the run. And I'm still the executive type, with twelve sisters serving in the print shop. They proof copy, set type, run the same old presses, cut stencils, handle mailings, and perform a hundred other essential chores. The magazine is the big effort, but there's also a newsletter and an annual calendar, plus all the outside work we can handle, such as stationery, school journals, programs, and announcements. Only faith keeps the presses rolling. They must be older than the magazine, founded in 1888. I may be the only one around who worries about them, and I dread the day when one or the other has to be replaced. A single press costs over a hundred thousand dollars these days, and where do you find money like that? I mean, it doesn't grow on trees. It seemed to, when I was helping to raise those millions for the village, but I can't seem to raise ten cents for a new press.

That hurts, because new equipment would mean that we could triple our circulation, to say nothing of the work load. Overhead wouldn't increase. The sister labor, for example, is not unionized. And triple income would mean that much more for the blind. But the labor force is against replacing the presses. "That's no way to treat old friends," I've been told many times.

As it has for so many years, the *Messenger and Advocate* continues to support the two hundred elderly residents of St. Joseph's Home for the Blind and St. Joseph's School for the Blind, where fifty sisters and lay experts provide care and teaching for over two hundred disturbed blind children. Those are the children I now visit in my free time. The school is about three miles from the convent and print shop.

So that's life as it goes today for one sister of St. Joseph's. I'm making good and concentrating in one area, more or less. The area under the sky.

And I'm feeling more and more in tune with the world. Renewal is just great, and sooner or later all of us, including the slow learners, will embrace it. It's so infectious:

"You're forever talking renewal," said Sister Coordinator, formerly known as Mother Superior, "and you were among the first to wear the short habit and you have a fondness for contemporary clothes, but what about your hair?"

It was two inches shorter than it had been the day before. I told her so.

"I noticed. Did you cut it yourself?"

"No. Sister Beatrice cut it for me."

"I suppose I could have guessed that," said Sister Director. She studied my head and shook hers as she added, "Sister Beatrice's talent hasn't improved."

It was more than a hint. That very day, I visited a beauty shop in Jersey City. I hadn't been inside one in over twenty years. "Do something for me," I told the hairdresser. He knew me. His wife was one of our Friday volunteers at the village.

"Any idea as to just what you want?" he asked.

"Not a one. Just give me something that suits me," I told him. Then I watched his reflection in the mirror. He was studying the shape of my head and the texture of my hair.

"Is this dark red natural?"

"Natural in a gradual sense," I said. "It was closer to fire-red years ago."

"All right, here goes. Would you mind closing your eyes.

I went to parochial schools when I was a kid, and I still get nervous when a nun watches me."

I closed my eyes.

When I opened them again, at his direction, my hairdo had been styled and renewed. Not much hair was left.

"Do you like it? It's the Mia Farrow cut."

I liked it. It didn't make me look Mia's age, but I liked it. As the saying goes, it did something for me.

When Sister Director next saw me, she asked, "Sister Beatrice again?"

"No, I went to a professional. It's actually shaped to my head."

"Now isn't that interesting?"

"And it has a name," I told her. "This is the Mia Farrow cut."

"How nice. The what cut?"

"The Mia Farrow cut," I explained again. "You know, Frank Sinatra."

"Oh. And who is he?"

5

The Questions People Ask

With apologies to the Boy Scouts, "Be Prepared" are the only two words of advice I give to our newly arrived junior professed nuns. Whenever they are outside the convent walls, they must be prepared to answer all sorts of questions about the life they lead. Curiosity is a part of human nature, and that, I suppose, is why film fan magazines were born. At this very minute, tens of thousands of people are eager to know if space pilots in space feel closer to God, if a certain screen siren sleeps in the raw, and if any foods are off limits for nuns. I am qualified only to answer the one about foods: none, and I'm mad about pickled eggs, kugelhof, and gefilte fish.

Five years ago, the questions asked were infrequent and most came on paper, as sort of asides, in letters devoted to other subjects. "Please accept my apologies if this is out of order, but I've been wondering if a nun ever has a vacation?" for example. Yes, if anyone is still wondering.

But these days, the questions are more likely to be asked in person. This is a result of renewal. We are more exposed to the public, and thus more available, and no longer considered isolated-from-the-world women.

So the answering of questions has become a part of my life's story. The questions haven't always seemed relevant to me, and you can be sure that I often follow up by asking questions of my own. Nuns, too, can be curious, and we believe in equal rights.

These questions and answers constitute a sampler from my memory book:

"Did you vote for me?"

The year was 1960, the place was West Point, and the questioner was President John F. Kennedy. "I did," I assured him, "and I almost wore out my knees praying as the electoral count mounted on television." I didn't tell him that the walls of my office were covered with his pictures, cut from magazines. But I did show him the button I'd worn under my bib all during his campaign. It carried these words: "If I were twenty one, I'd vote for Jack." He laughed and asked me to show it to others in his official party. We'll never see the likes of him again.

"And what do you think of Jacqueline?"
Still one of the most frequent questions (mostly asked by women), and I wish it were otherwise. What should one think? She has her life, and she should be able to live it according to her will and not that of the press, magazines, and spectators. God watches over Greece as well as America.

"So you vote, but do you pay taxes?"
Until recently, the answer was "No" or "Pay taxes on what?" but now we have to hedge a bit. Nuns of some orders, including mine, are now permitted to hold non-religious, salaried jobs, live away from the convent, become regular members of their new community, and help lay people as the needs arise. When their incomes qualify them for federal and state taxes, they pay them. And as with anyone else, there's a limit on the charitable gifts they can deduct. Any savings that remain after living expenses are met are sent to the order for its continuing needs.

"But do you think its normal for a woman not to marry?"
Another popular question, and often it's asked by a successful career woman. There are some ten million unmarried career women in the United States, and only a million nuns in the entire world. Sometimes, it seems to me that the wrong people are asking the question. But be that as it

may, my answer is always a firm "Yes," and that usually stops the conversation.

"What do you think about the lay fashions based on the monk's robe, the nun's habit, the cardinal's dress, and the pontifical hat?"
Well, it's a fair interchange. Since some sisters wear lay clothes much of the time, it's high time the fashion designers recognized the religious styles. Indeed, we'd be even happier if more designers, models, and consumers borrowed more of our ideas. We'd love to see them all in church.

"Did you say you liked baseball?"
Almost as much as horse racing is what I told pitcher Jim Bouton. We were sitting next to each other at a dinner attended by sports celebrities. The Yankees weren't doing so well (they had lost again that day), and Mr. Bouton was in a sour mood. He wasn't friendly until after I'd delivered my speech. Then he told me that while he didn't like women speakers, what I'd said about the village had impressed him, and he felt better about life. I suppose he meant that it was better to be a losing Yankee than an orphan. Then we started talking baseball, and he wondered if his team would ever win. I told him to pray, and that I would round up additional support. The next morning, I asked thirty of our children to pray for the Yankees to win. They did, and the Yankees lost. Then the Yankees took off on a four-game winning streak. Just delayed action, I thought, but I was wrong. A ten-year-old confessed: "I'm sorry, Sister, but I really prayed for the Red Sox in the morning. Then

I felt guilty, so I prayed for the Yankees that night."
Unanimity is sometimes necessary.

"Why are nuns permitted to solicit contributions in bars?"
Ladies dressed in long habits are not always nuns. Costumes
are easily rented or made. One of these days we'll be blamed
for the perfect bank robbery. Take if from me, nuns are
never found in bars.

"Why do nuns travel in pairs?"
Because they are headed in the same direction. There's no
set rule about traveling in pairs or by the dozen. I drive
about fifteen thousand miles a year, for example, and I'm
often alone. Am I capable of changing a flat tire? Yes, but
I would like to thank the truck drivers of America for
helping me on almost every occasion. Other drivers usually
whiz by. I guess a nun by the side of a road must look like a
suspicious character, or else the average driver doesn't know
how to change tires. I might add here that in a certain
Michigan city, some high echelon people call me the Dusty
Green Chevy Nun.

"What's the source of your lay clothes?"
Until recently, we had to depend on family, relatives, and
friends. If not for the clothes, then the materials for same.
So the handier the sister was with a needle, the more re-
splendent her wardrobe. Naturally, I was always at a dis-
advantage. Sisters working at salaried jobs on the outside,
of course, were able to purchase at least some parts of their
wardrobes. Things, however, have changed in my order

and we are granted small clothing allowances. Of course, one's entire annual allowance could easily be spent on a single dress, so the trend is still toward do-it-yourself.

"Do you still have strict rules of dress?"
Dress is pretty much a matter of personal choice between the traditional habit, the modified habit, and contemporary clothes. I don't think it will be many years before the long habit disappears entirely. It's neither a comfortable nor a practical form of dress. Something that swishes along the ground has to require frequent laundering and ironing.

"The pill?"
This seems to be today's popular question, and quite often it comes from husbands, over the phone. One head of an abundant family said, "Sister, we must use the pill in order to survive. What shall we do?" I told him, as I tell all others, to follow his conscience. I don't encourage or discourage. In the long run, people interpret laws to suit their own convenience. The man going fifty miles an hour in a posted thirty-mile zone thinks when arrested that the cop was hiding illegally behind the bush.

"Were you disappointed in love?"
No. And someday I'll ask the same of the apparently happily married questioner.

"Are nuns eligible for Social Security?"
Yes.

"Are the sisters permitted to accept gifts?"

Yes, if the gifts are within reason. Except for the sisters holding salaried jobs outside the religious community, ready cash isn't always available for the purchase of personal wants. Almost always, the sisters' cameras, radios, and (these days) articles of fashion arrived as gifts from their families or friends, and sometimes from strangers. There are times when the gift givers get a bit wild. In the recent past, I was offered a pet ocelot. Among my own unexpected gifts have been an electric knife (it went to our kitchen staff), a deluxe toy train set (it went to our children), and a telescope (it also went to the children). Some years ago, and about three months after I had talked at an annual dinner of a towel company, fifteen hundred bath towels arrived out of the blue. Oh, that was a great day! The convent was running short on towels.

"I can't recall seeing a sister at the movies. Don't you ever go?"

During the BPJ* age, we were permitted to see certain films (*The Bells of St Mary's*, for example), but only when the show was held specifically for the sisters. In this new APJ age, we may see any film (time permitting) at any regular showing, selection being a matter of good taste. Our habits are a great advantage when we go to the theater, for the management doesn't always charge us. Often, too, you are seeing sisters at the movies, but you don't recognize them. Any attractive young ladies down the aisle from you—without male escorts—might be sisters who are not wearing the traditional habits.

* Before Pope John.

"Do you have any political advice?"

The questioner was Judge Richard Hughes. "Show more enthusiasm," I told him. He did, and three months later he was Governor Richard Hughes of New Jersey. Later, at a dinner where I was last on the menu, he told the audience about that brief conversation and confessed, "It was the first time I was ever put in my place by a sister." Except for gamblers, enthusiasm is essential for success.

"Can one person do anything to help progress in the world?"

Yes. Love your neighbor.

"Is there a minimum age for women wishing to enter the convent?"

No, but requirements for candidates have changed drastically over the last few years, and about 45 percent of all applicants are accepted as postulants. Most have college degrees, or at least two years of college, or several years of business experience. Old enough, mature enough, and experienced enough to now the reality of total commitment. Entering a convent to save one's soul is now considered an outdated, selfish, neurotic idea. Still, many young women cling to it, as psychological testing continues to reveal. Constructive, creative, aware candidates are needed. Strange as it may seem to some people, some of the hippies have the right ideas, but they're going in the wrong direction.

"Was Teilhard de Chardin right? Can we correlate science with God?"

Why not? Just remember Who created science.

"How many black sisters do you have in St. Joseph's?"
None, but also there have never been any black applicants
for our novitiate, where race and color are not barriers.
Any woman in a state of good mental and physical health
and with the required educational background is welcome
to apply. Of the 400,000 nuns in the United States, only
about 1,000 are black. Most, but not all, belong to all-black
orders; we continue to hope and work to change this.

"Are you permitted to drink?"
Yes, but I don't think you'll ever see a nun wearing the
traditional habit in a cocktail lounge. Before entering the
sisterhood, several of our sisters learned how to mix a fine
dry martini, and they haven't lost the talent. At our home,
we usually have beer in the refrigerator. Drinking is neither
frowned upon nor encouraged.

"Do the sisters have a favorite television program?"
I don't, but in my visits to convents around the country I've
noticed that Saturday nights are called Lawrence Welk
Nights.

"Are you permitted to become involved in politics?"
Indeed we are, and we've been encouraged to do so since
APJ. We do vote, we do want to be a part of the scene, and
we do want to understand everybody, including politicians.
On the other hand, we'll never run for elected offices. That
would be a bit much for the public to handle, I think.

"Do you visit beauty parlors and do you wear curlers?"

As the night follows day, so curlers follow hair stylings that call for them. But one way to tell a nun dressed in street clothes from any other woman is to look at her hairdo. If it's wired for sound, the lady is not a nun.

"What do you think of him?"

A stranger asked the question on a night in Yankee Stadium as we watched the distant figure of Pope Paul. While he was not in the tradition of John, I thought he had already established himself as one of the greatest men of our times, and events have since proven that conclusion. Who else has devoted himself so intensely to the cause of world peace, and has given so much of himself in bringing his message to distant peoples? And yet, if I had been granted a single moment to talk to him, I think I would have said, "Your Holiness, one thing you've overlooked thus far is the rising hour for nuns. We still suffer medieval mornings." I was close to him later, but refrained. He seemed so very, very tired.

"How about smoking?"

I suppose that some nuns do smoke, but I doubt that you'll ever see a nun smoking in public. People just won't accept that image. I smoked a bit in my Madison Avenue days, gave it up long before I entered the novitiate, and haven't had the urge since. Why some people can't give up smoking is beyond me. It requires an absolute minimum of willpower.

"Wouldn't it be better if sisters had stayed the way they were?"

Now I can tell anyone who asks that question to read this book.

"Are sisters really relevant in today's society?"

Yes, but not in the old pattern.

"Will religious life exist twenty-five years from now?"

Religious life will never go out of style, but it can't very well continue in the structural sense of today. I think religious life will dwindle down to a nucleus and from that nucleus will emerge leadership for a new type of religious life that will be free to concentrate wherever needed. Global changes, technological changes are inevitable, and religious life will try to keep pace.

"Must you always stay in a convent when you're away from your own?"

Not anymore. There was a time when we couldn't stay overnight with our families, or in any private home. Those days are gone forever.

"Should sisters take part in public demonstrations?"

We can, and some do. It's a matter of one's personal convictions.

"Do you have a set time for relaxation?"

No. And this question usually leads to one about our physical exercise. Most of the sisters indulge in Ping-Pong, tennis, softball, swimming, and jogging. I prefer bowling, and may never top 200. In my average week, however, there's only time for the twist board. One of these days I intend to get back to riding. The long habit wasn't designed for the saddle.

"Are you free to come and go when not on assignment?"

Yes, if we have the strength.

"How are sisters received as teachers in public schools?"

Haven't heard any complaints to date. They are addressed as "Miss" and absolutely do not try to sell religion to the students. For those with Emily Post on their minds, it's perfectly proper to introduce a sister as "Miss" if she is wearing contemporary dress. She won't be embarrassed, but the gentleman one introduces her to might be if he asks for a date. All this is in keeping with Pope John's edict that we become individuals.

"Why are some sisters giving up their religious names for their own baptismal names?"

This gives true validity to the sacrament of baptism. Further, we lose an identity we don't really need, and in the losing gain stronger membership in the world community.

"Is Pope Paul dragging his feet?"

Read about what he's been doing for world peace and you must conclude that the world is dragging its feet.

"What is the meaning of Community?"
A group dedicated to serving people, and to living in an atmosphere of respect and love. Not an easy atmosphere to achieve, by the way, for the sisters are only human. The sharing, the close living, the acceptance of others for what they are, the mutual respect and tolerance—all contribute to tensions that must build but are somehow always kept under wraps.

"Was the traditional life more stable before Pope John?"
It was more rote. All thinking was done for us. Now we have thinking sisters, mature and able enough to shoulder responsibilities on their own. And to my mind, thinking does not interfere with stability.

"Do guitars and folk Masses reflect the spirit of the Church?"
Why not? The Church is the people and the people are reflected by their music. Among my favorites are "Blowin' in the Wind," "Sons of God," and "We Are Over the Land."

"What happens to sisters who leave the convent life for private lives as lay people?"
We correspond with them all, help some to secure jobs, and support others while they seek employment. Many are happily married.

"Are sisters permitted to go abroad to pursue higher education?"

Yes. Support is the problem, of course. Grants, scholarships, and loans are the usual ways of finding that support.

"The color of your eyes?"
Blue-gray.
My weight? Steady.
Diet? Never.

Yes, people do ask personal questions. I think it's a sure sign that we're succeeding, that the mystique is vanishing, that we're being accepted by more and more people as just regular human beings.

Not everybody asks, of course. That will take a little time.

One of our sisters works as a public-school teacher in a poor section of Manhattan. She wears contemporary clothes, but everybody in the neighborhood knows that she's a nun.

On a very hot day, Sister Ruth walked along a sidewalk lined with stairs leading to faded front doors. On the lower steps of one tenement, a man sat watching her. He was naked to the waist and held a can of beer in one hand. As she came along, Sister Ruth exchanged greetings with him.

"Get rid of that can of beer!" the man's wife shouted from an open window. "Even a slob like you should have better sense! What will Sister Ruth think of you? Would you chew tobacco in front of Jesus?"

The man put the beer can on the steps beside him.

Sister Ruth picked up the can and handed it back to him.

"It's not a sin to seek relief from the heat," she told him. "I envy you, but I just can't stand the taste of beer."

She smiled and walked away, and the wife in the window shouted, "And you call yourself a nun?"

Yes, people ask all sorts of questions.

6

Reflections of a Contemporary Nun

A love of God and all that He made.
That's my basic philosophy of life, and how I wish that a few others would embrace it. Millions do and millions more will, of course, but not the few I'm talking about. They are the ones who stand ready to blow the world apart, if they don't get their candy.

I debate with them in my dreams, and they always say something like, "But, Sister, why are you complaining? We love what He made. Who else created the atom?" Yes, but He had something else in mind, and he certainly did not split it!

This is a dangerous age and it could be a wonderful age. Love, or respect, what He made. Nations, people, neighbors. The best example is the Peace Corps. We aren't trying to ram the American way of life down the throats of those needy people. We're helping them to improve their own way of life, and that's love with respect. A century from now, if people are still around and still reading, they'll be reading about St. Shriver.

The worst example, in this country anyway, is the Ku Klux Klan. Some people argue for the Mafia, but as I understand it, the Mafia's only prejudice is against the law. I hate to admit it, but almost everyone has the same prejudice. The law is for the other fellow, the parking ticket was granted by a crooked cop, and the draft is for the other mother's son. I hate to admit it because I'm an honorary member of the New York City Police Department, and I believe in law and order. Society can exist without both, but not a democratic society.

Love all that He made. It means respect and tolerance for everyone one knows and meets: high or low, poor or rich, maddening or cooperative, eager or stupid, your race and creed or otherwise. It means understanding and helping, and the end result is happiness.

I didn't find happiness. One day I looked around and discovered happiness pursuing me. The moment it caught me I lost my last little doubt and knew that I was in the only right profession for me.

That phrase about the pursuit of happiness is the only real

argument I have with the Constitution. One does not pursue happiness. It is the other way around.

To an unfortunate and great degree, the pursuit of happiness remains an American way of life. I think this is more true for women than for men, and certainly true for the women in suburbia. To their husbands, happiness means career success. To the ladies, happiness is the material: the latest-model car, the newest in freezers and television, today's fashions. Not just keeping up with the Joneses, but staying ahead of the Joneses. While proud of their husbands and children, they are happiest when their mates bring home more of the bacon, so that the family debt can be increased, and when their children are going steady at the ages of eleven and twelve.

All this, of course, isn't happiness. It's pseudo-happiness, at best. The end result of this easy living is boredom, and this infection leads to many things: the bottle, the psychiatric ward, divorce, and sometimes suicide. The statistics are available, and they prove that wives fail more often in suburbia than in the city or on the farm. That may be why so many husbands insist on moving back to the city when the children have flown the nest.

Is there a cure for boredom? Yes, but it's not found in drinking, flirting, shopping, complaining, or on the psychiatric couch. It's found in daily personal reflection, and it doesn't cost a penny. The only other name for this cure is introspection.

Women by the thousands have told me that they don't have time for introspection. They seem to think that only women who live in convents can find such time, and that, of course, is nonsense. In her average day, any woman can find ten minutes for introspection, although the finding may mean such sacrifices as not making a gossipy phone call, not watching television, not reading beauty hints in a favorite magazine, or instructing junior to walk home from school—if it's not raining. Of course, those are supreme sacrifices. Maybe it's easier to arise ten minutes earlier in the morning. The end of the day is not the right time for introspection. It means another lost day.

"And just how do I introspect?" I'm often asked by women, as if the word were obsolete, and sometimes it does seem that way. "A private, personal, meaningful analysis of yourselves," I've learned to tell them. "Meaningful" and "analysis" are two of the most overused words in the English language, and they are understood by almost everybody.

Still, that explanation isn't sufficient for some. They must be told just what to analyze, and I tell them to start asking questions and giving honest answers, no matter how much it hurts. "What is my investment in others?" is always a good starter. The investment starts with family, reaches out to community, and stretches beyond to strangers in the world. This investment pays dividends for those who can scuttle their personal ships of social, racial, color, and religious prejudices.

That's often an embarrassing question for a woman to ask herself. So, "Am I really a woman of stature?" is a reasonable substitute. This doesn't mean being a member of the jet set, or wearing the most expensive clothes, or belonging to the hunt club, or being the only person on the street to subscribe to seventeen English magazines. It means being accepted as a human being of quality, constructive in every possible way. The common rebuttal is usually, "But I don't care what people think of me, so long as Harry approves."

Nonsense. Everybody wants to be accepted as the right kind of a human being. Even Harry looks beyond his ever-loving wife.

I've heard Harry speak a couple of hundred times. "I accept this great honor in all modesty," he proclaims, holding aloft the gold medallion. "I say modesty, because I'm not forgetting for one minute that I wouldn't be standing here right now if it weren't for my wife. Where are you, Ella? Will you stand up, please? Yes, ladies and gentlemen, this award really belongs to Ella. I'm here to tell you that at least one axiom still rings true: 'Behind every successful man stands a woman!' That has most certainly been true in my case."

I never did buy that axiom. I've been around suburbia too much, and known too many successful men and their loving wives. I think the key to their success was the long commute. It gave them time for introspection.

"Did you mean that?" I once asked a successful Harry.

"Mean what?"

"The tribute to your wife?"

"I cannot tell a lie to you, Sister," said Harry. "I knew what I was going to say, but I didn't expect you to be at the speaker's table. So when I saw you there, I thought about changing my acceptance speech. Then I decided that the axiom wasn't a lie in my case. You see, I'm a company man, and even a whisper of scandal would have ruined me." He paused and smiled, as if wondering whether it would be proper to continue or not. "I hope this won't shake you, Sister, but my wife knew about every one of my mistresses, and she never spilled the beans. So she really did stand by me. Are you shook?"

I was unshook.

Months before I entered the novitiate, my father left
Manhattan for greener fields. For a while he kept in
touch with my brother, and so he was aware that I was entering the convent. And later, my brother informed him that I
was at St. Michael's.

I wrote to my father several times, but never received a
word in reply. Then my letters started coming back to me,
stamped "Address Unknown." At the same time, he stopped
writing to my brother.

When last heard from, many years ago, my father was in
Florida. It made good sense, for to him the greenest pastures
were those surrounding race tracks. We tried to locate him
and failed.

The years rolled along. He was always in my prayers, but
my prayers remained unanswered until this summer when an
old family friend—really the daughter of the old friend—
phoned me from Manhattan. "Sit down and listen," she said.
"I have a surprise for you. A man just telephoned and asked
for your address. He said he was your father."

"Where can I find him?"

"He gave me an address in Manhattan. Got a pencil?"

It was late afternoon. I tried to phone, but information had
no number listed for the address. Then I sent a wire to him advising that I would be there at noon on the next day.

In the evening, another call came from my friend Agnes.
"I went to the address, and guess what?" "Tell me." It was a
large apartment house and your father wasn't listed in the di-
rectory in the lobby so I sought out the superintendent. He

didn't know anyone named Quin. Not even one with a double n."

"Did you describe my father?"

"How could I? I haven't seen him in twenty years." Eighteen really. I told her I would be on the scene the next day anyway. She offered to accompany me, but she didn't offer encouragement. "We don't even know if the man who called is your father. All we know is that he doesn't live at that address. I'm beginning to think the whole thing is a hoax. For some reason, somebody wants to get you into the city at that address! If you insist on going, I think we should have police protection!"

I vetoed that idea. I felt sure it had been my father and Agnes believed that the best American writing is found in murder novels.

The next morning, I drove through the Holland Tunnel and as luck would have it, a truck broke down and held up traffic forty-five agonizing minutes. As I was waiting in the tunnel I kept thinking: Wonder how Dad looks after eighteen years. What will he think of me in my Nun's habit? Is he well? What has he been doing?

We reached the address a little before noon. It was a large apartment complex and I realized that without an apartment number it might be a little like trying to find a needle in a haystack. Back to the superintendent. "Can I help you, Sister?" He was not the man Agnes had talked to the night before. This one really was the superintendent, the man the night before was a helper.

"I'm looking for a man named John Quin. One n."

"Young or old?"

"Over seventy. Do you know him? He gave this place as his address."

"Sorry, Sister, he is not a tenant but he might be boarding with one of them or even visiting. I'll keep my eye out just in case I see a man who fits your dad's description."

Just as I walked to the door to leave I heard the elevator open and there was my father.

My father was standing just inside the door. He was staring at me. He grinned, and I started to cry.

"Just like a woman," he said.

Within a few hours, and over his strenuous objections, he was in a hospital. He didn't have the strength to put up much of a fight. Malnutrition and tuberculosis had played havoc with him.

He responded to care, and these days his address is a home for the elderly. But he insists that he's not ready to retire and busies himself with odd jobs around the place. I see him every week and keep him supplied with his favorite reading material: biographies, mysteries, and books about horses.

In the hospital, nurses, interns, and doctors were fascinated by his knowledge and advice. Some did very well at the tracks, and that pleased him. "You aren't the only member of the family to help the needy," he told me many times.

I thought it best to warn the officials at the home about his enthusiasm for the bangtails. "It was a terrible thing to do!" he scolded me. "Three widows here have already made fortunes on paper. If it weren't for you, they'd be busting out of here and taking me South where we could live in the sun and clean up." He calmed down a bit when I made arrangements for him to buy one New York State lottery ticket a month, but he still grumbles about the odds. And he derives pleasure from introducing me as "This is my Sister Vincent, or my daughter, who is not my sister."

He's seventy-eight now and celebrates his birthday on Christmas Eve. "When you get to know me well, you'll realize I was born a few hours early," he's fond of telling religious people.

His son, my brother, continues to live in the San Francisco area. We see each other about every two years. Bill is still in the liquor business, and a happy family man.

"There's never been a family act like those two," my father tells people. "My daughter is in the business of curing sinners, and my son is in the business of supplying her."

In the long run, I don't think the pill or anything else will serve to limit the world's population. Despite wars, famines, plagues, other great disasters, and even common sense, there are more people on earth at the end of each year than at the beginning. It's been that way for a long time, there's no relief in sight, and there never will be. For every team of limitation thinkers, there are five teams working on health and longevity.

I have nothing against the population explosion except that we have enough needy people in the world right now, nobody is really helping millions of them, and there will be millions more tomorrow.

One doesn't have to look far to find the needy. One finds them wherever he looks in this, the most prosperous land in the world. No matter who the "ins" have been, Washington has always been aware of this and has constantly increased the federal appropriations. It's a matter of money, and the money spent thus far hasn't put much of a dent in poverty. That's growing all the time, and at a faster rate than tax dollars.

Of course, the needy aren't Washington's only concern. There's the problem of getting to the moon, for example. How many loaves of bread and pairs of shoes and schoolbooks would one spaceship buy? A friend of mine with Pentagon contacts insists that the whole moon program is defeatist and immoral. The plot, according to him, is to create living conditions up there, transport the affluent part of our society, and leave the poverty part right where it is. So there would be no needy in the moon civilization.

The friend, a leading theologian who is not of my faith, feels that the government will never be able to erase the poverty problem. Not alone, anyway. It needs help. The Church must play a more active role.

"With what?" I asked him.

"With people and money."

The Church, and here the term Church embraces all religions, can always find people. Money is a different matter. That was the rub.

"Not so difficult as you might think," he advised. "Do you think it matters to the Lord whether we worship Him in a cathedral or in an open field?"

In other words, stop building new churches. Apply the money saved to help our neighbors. If this theory is accepted, hundreds of millions of dollars—and billions over the years—could be found today to help in the fight against poverty.

I'm for it, and I think only those who think of worship as the fashionable, respectable thing to do will object. And it gives me a warm feeling to read now and then that others who are really important are for it, too. *Really important* because they've vetoed plans for a new church building and are spending the money where it matters. I hope this idea catches on and that we'll see the day when people gather to worship in all sorts of shrines: fields and parking lots, theaters and stadiums, barns and armories, school auditoriums and athletic fields.

Some people won't get the message. They won't approve. But the Lord will approve, and He's the one who matters.

The great difference between today's crop of sisters and the veteran and frayed, such as myself, is in their approach to duty. They are dedicated to His service, but are not content to serve in the old traditional and structured manners. They want to serve in their own ways, in accordance with their own personalities and convictions, and they do.

They don't object to waxing the convent's floors or fulfilling other necessary chores, but their hearts and minds are elsewhere—out in the world where the less fortunate need their sympathy and help. No whispering for them. They talk as they work, exchanging ideas, discussing new approaches to problems, and worried about the time spent on waxing. I haven't seen a professional wax job in three years.

The newcomers radiate enthusiasm. It's in their eyes, their laughter, and even the way they walk. Their counterparts are found on every college campus, and one can't help wondering why so many have chosen the convent over marriage, or the airlines, or—in the case of the genuine beauties—modeling or films. Their answers are always the same: a spiritual life seemed the fullest life, and they have found it so. Easy to understand, but so difficult to explain. It's an inner something. There are no precise words.

This go-go-go generation of nuns was conditioned differently from the way mine was, of course. In my day at St. Michael's, we didn't even think of wearing slacks behind locked doors. We knew about hi-fi, but never heard its tones. We attended Mass or else, but today only two Masses are on the weekly schedule in the chapel, and postulants may attend them or others elsewhere. Sit-ins, folk Masses, pop records, guitars, nonreligious books, odd signs on doors, college pennants on walls, crazy pillows, talk-talk-talk, visiting lecturers on many subjects—well, the novitiate isn't a college dormitory, but sometimes it seems that way. Holy cards and other signs of packaged spirituality aren't in evidence anymore. In terms of renewal, my old home is probably ahead of the convent. If I had my life to lead over again, I'd head straight back to St. Michael's.

Today the novices who succeed and become junior professed nuns are swinging with the new times and acting as if our world had always been this way. I know that we're in the middle of a revolution, for I came along just in time to know the old ways and help usher in the new. There will be more changes in the future, and these new ones will adjust with ease and take them in stride. They won't hold long discussions about how far to go. They'll just go. Two years from now, if they can restrain themselves that long, most will be wearing short habits in seasonal colors. *When* they wear habits, I mean.

The one problem with the new sisters is that there aren't enough of them. As the number of hopeful candidates for the novitiate swells, the percentage of acceptances falls. Educational requirements are now higher, and then there's the new psychological screening. We are getting the quality, but not in sufficient numbers. So the supply isn't meeting the demand, and often there isn't a new replacement to fill the gap created by the elderly nun who is no longer strong enough to remain active.

Hopefully, this picture will change in the near future. Meanwhile, a great deal of thought is being driven to the creation of a sort of auxiliary corps. It would be composed of women who would enter His service for a set period of time or for an indefinite number of years. Some might seek a nun's role as a means of personal rehabilitation, others because they want to devote a part but not all of their life to the Lord. They would not be required to take the final vows, nor would they be under any pressure to do so. But they would be nuns in every other sense while remaining with us. My own hunch is that the auxiliary nun, under that or any other name, will be a part of my order within the next year. We know and the Lord knows that we need more hands. There's always more work to be done than time permits.

Ten years ago, this sort of thinking about bringing short-term sisters into the fold would have been considered radical. Today it's routine. Just another part of renewal.

If there had never been a Pope John, and if he had never opened the windows, I would still be dusting chairs in the convent. He wasn't just a man for all seasons, he was a man for all times.

I suppose everybody knows he was a sort of interim selection. An elderly, pastoral, fatherly kind of man who wasn't expected to do much more than carry on the traditional assignments and ceremonies of his high office. His wit was well established, but his wisdom would come as a surprise. Those who knew him well called him a humorist, but not an intense one. He thought nothing of enjoying a drink in public, or of visiting his own blood relatives in prison. They regarded him as a simple and good man, but not as a deep thinker. A normal human being.

How wrong they were. Not about his being a normal human, for he was more normal than any of the Popes who had served before him, but as to his not being a deep thinker. He was the first to see through the frills of centuries, and to eliminate them. He was the first to articulate the need for involvement at every level: Church, State, community, and individual.

John preached love, peace, and humanity as few men ever had. He encouraged average men and women, and the above average, too, to look around and open their eyes and help their fellows, high and low. And above all, he brought the Church into modern times. He was the inventor of renewal.

It has been said (and I was the one who said it, to a group of insurance salesmen) that the Church goes rocking and floating down the centuries, always imperfect and seeming to get nowhere at all. Just another ark that makes for no obvious harbor, having only the task of staying afloat until the waters subside, so that drowning men can be helped aboard.

Pope John added lifeboats to that ark, placed a skilled navigator aboard, and installed radar. Today the ark just doesn't float around, waiting for something to happen. It heads for where the action is.

Hope, faith, and love were the basics John taught us, and not enough people were listening. Not even those at the

United Nations. There they did heed his call for involvement, but have been practicing it too little and often too late.

He knew, of course, that Christian life will always be an uphill carrying of the Cross in search of a world with the fewest possible imperfections, and that the Promised Land will always be where it is right now—over the hills and far away. Still, we must always head in that direction. There is no other choice.

I just can't understand all this noise about a generation gap. It's too tidy an excuse for a family state of affairs that's really delinquency at two levels.

There are the adult delinquents, better known as parents, who seem to feel that the responsibility battle is almost won the moment the cigars are passed around and the child has been baptized. From there on, they give the child all the good, material things in life as fast as the things are invented and the bankroll permits. It's as if school and Church are Junior's real parents. If he's going to learn anything about life, he learns it in those places. This is parental responsibility?

Few people run from the easy life, and running never crosses Junior's mind. He doesn't have to break a law to become a delinquent. He was born as one, and he accepts "the better world than ours" his parents have given him because he's too immature to know better. Getting what he wants and never earning it, looking for trouble when he doesn't get what he wants, considering discipline to be an un-American word —that's Junior's way of life. He's never heard of responsibility, either.

Listen. The poor families—and I mean the really poor—

have two generations under one roof, too. They work when they can find work, share when they have something to share, and worry about tomorrow and not a better way of life. Now some of them steal because that's a pretty good way to find money to buy food; but when Junior gets caught by the police, his father beats the daylights out of him. That's discipline. If Junior isn't responsible enough to steal, he shouldn't try it.

The whole point here is that there's no generation gap among the poor. It's tough when you don't have enough, but it's a sin when you have too much and don't know how to handle it.

There are times when I'm grateful to the hippies. They helped me warm up many an audience.

After a little experience, a public speaker is able to sense an audience's mood. Those seas of strange faces can be eager to listen, or wait-and-see, or almost openly hostile. It's the hostile sea that worries me. I feel a chill as I stand in response to the introduction and wait for the scattered, polite applause to diminish.

The chill comes on strongest in suburbia, where my audiences are usually all female. I suppose the girls are thinking, "If it weren't for Elliot, I might be she. Wow!"

Thus far, this hippie story—served as an opener—has always brought them over to my side:

Two male hippies are walking down the street. Approaching them is a priest, his right arm in a sling.

As the three come close, Hippie One asks of the priest, "What happened to you, man?" The priest explains that he slipped in the bathtub and fractured his arm. Then he continues on his way.

"What's a bathtub?" asked Hippie Two.

"How should I know?" says Hippie One. "I'm not a Catholic."

Well, that's the story, and I figure the few ladies who don't laugh are probably the mothers of hippies.

G od created men as equals long before America promised to make them so. I think of that every time I see a picture of an elected official taking the oath of office with his right hand placed upon the Bible.

Equality means racial equality these days. We call it civil rights. A polite term for doing something about racism.

Pope John had racism in mind when he preached involvement. I suppose he hoped the churches of the world, the religious people of the world, would lead the way in wiping out the ugly word and its meaning.

Not all the religious have responded, but many have. Their ranks will swell. On my level, and now that we have some voice in our assignments, more and more sisters are working full time in both the ghetto areas and the affluent white communities.

White communities? Why not. Somebody has to confront the white individuals and institutions. That's what racism is all about. Its color is white.

W e've learned a few things about children at the village, where sisters must play dual roles—as mothers and fathers.

163

Viz.: As with puppies, the children of one family don't always develop at the same rate. We deal with the children of many families and find great diversification in any given age bracket. There are fast learners and slow ones, for example, and it's best to plan separate school and work programs for both. The more subtle the planning, the more resultant the harmony between the groups.

Viz.: Even with the best of intentions and the highest administrative skills, no institution can really substitute for family life. There's no true home-away-from-home in a child's mind. The more contact the growing child has with normal family life, the more stable his personality. That's why we encourage our children to accept invitations from the right kinds of families on holidays, weekends, and vacations. The samplings are beacons for their own futures.

Viz.: Sex is a question but never a problem, and it seems to preoccupy the girls at an earlier age than the boys. We can and do prevent pornographic literature from invading the premises, but this doesn't hinder normal curiosity or—in the case of the older children who are bussed off to public schools and meet new associates—a sort of stimulated curiosity. While we don't hold lectures on the subject, every child knows we'll answer any and all questions. Thus an honest question gets an appropriate answer. For obvious reasons, the city child asks more questions than the farm child. The latter has more understanding and a normal view. More families should be reared on farms.

Viz.: Overall, the children who go off to public school are better-adjusted individuals than those who, for one reason or another, must receive their education on the village's premises. Association with other children from all levels of society keeps them in touch with the real world, and the envy they feel for their new friends from happy homes isn't bitter. The haves can be moral lessons for the have-nots.

Viz.: The years from fourteen to eighteen are the most critical for the child. Within that span, his personality is set and his outlook formed. It's his most important period for normal family living, parental affection and guidance. That's why we make every effort to place our fourteen-year-olds with foster parents, and why I have my doubts about the private boarding-school system. I won't knock the educational advantages of those schools, but I doubt that they are adequate substitutes for home, affection, and guidance. It's the affluent society, of course, that keeps the private secondary schools going. And isn't that where the generation-gap business started?

Viz.: A child's capacity for learning is influenced by home environment. His heart isn't in his work if his mind remains on unhappy family problems. How can you instruct a child to forget? You can't. Lazy adults were born for each other, perhaps, but their marriage contract should include a vow to practice nonlazy birth control.

Viz.: Maturity does not improve one's stamina, and that's the real generation gap. For almost two years, I kept the same rough schedule as the children: identical times for rising, Mass, meals, school (they studied, I taught), and retiring at day's end. They thrived and I was exhausted. I trust there's a moral lesson in this experience for mothers. You can't outwait, outfight, or outlast your children. 'Tis wiser to outthink them.

Viz.: In any institution for children, group treatment is a must. There's not enough time for sufficient individual attention, and every child's development suffers. Hence, his full potential may never be realized.

Viz.: A child knows what an adult forgets—that money isn't everything. The youngster rates affection, attention, fun, and friends over material things.

Viz.: No matter what their background, all children are born critics. Here are a few comments from the ones I've known and loved, as reported to me or overheard by me:

"How could Sister Vincent know? She's a lady!"

"She's trying to brainwash us!"

"Listen, if she knew anything about the go-go set, she'd be on a diet."

"You shouldn't have asked her that question. Her father was a monk."

"The veil does more for her than she does for it."

"I love her better when she wears glasses. She reminds me of my grandfather."

"So then this waste of time tells me not to waste my time."

"Why should I respect her? She writes poetry."

"But I don't want an artificial mother."

Viz.: Never underestimate a child's awareness of the world. The monthly *Village Press Magazine* (two cents a copy), staffed and edited by the children, carried this editorial by a twelve-year-old girl:

> Stop to think—who will win the war? People say it's going to be a long, nasty war. That's why I ask you to stop and think. Our men over there can't wait for it to stop. People hope the war ends fast and we win and so do I. The men over there are so scared, they even shoot each other. So, I ask you to pray for them.

Over the past few years, I've corresponded with several soldiers on active service in Vietnam. The day after the editorial appeared, I received a letter from one of them. He had just arrived at a rest camp after several weeks in the field. "We all have the jitters, especially on patrols," he reported. "On a couple of nights, we ended up shooting at each other. How is Manhattan getting along without me? I must admit that I'm not always religious, Sister, but I get that way in a hurry when the shooting starts."

I think of myself as one of the safest drivers in the world, but this personal opinion is not shared by many of my lay friends. Still, I've never been in an accident, have always tried to keep within the designated speed limits and obey the lights, and nobody has ever driven off the road because of me. Obviously, my reputation as a reckless driver stems from association and thus is unfair.

The association itself is a false one. Public opinion holds that nuns in general just aren't safe behind the wheel. Jackie Farrell, the drum beater for the Yankees, put it this way: "If I could see five miles ahead and knew with certainty that no other car was coming my way, I would not pass a car with a nun at the wheel. Not even if she were doing ten miles an hour in a seventy-mile zone, as on the western plains, and the highway was an eight-laner."

Mr. Farrell is one of the most famous graduates of our old home for boys in Englewood Cliffs, the one that burned to the ground when I was a novice at St. Michael's. He's been good to us through the years and has helped us many, many times. No man is more devoted to St. Joseph's. So that's the special reason why sisters all over America cheer for the Yankees, and why it won't be long before that team wins a pennant again. We haven't been making enough noise to be heard above the din of the world's other troubles, but somebody up there will hear us someday. The press didn't mention why Pope Paul made his only public appearance in this country in Yankee Stadium, but we knew.

I laughed when Jackie made the statement, but not anymore. It reflected a national misconception. Friends and strangers have stated it in different ways, but this comes close to it: "Nuns drive as if the Lord were their unseen passenger," and we are sure that He always is.

The truth is that no other professional group in America has as safe a driving record as the nun group. Our record is amazing! Not a single arrest for drunken driving! Never an arrest for speeding! Keep in mind that we do not drive sporty or souped-up cars, we know how to concentrate, and we are conditioned to obeying laws, religious and otherwise. By the way, not every policeman is Irish.

I have been in four automobile accidents in my lifetime. Each time, a secular friend was at the wheel. The first time I asked, "Don't you think we're going too fast?"

"Not with you as a passenger," said my friend as she stepped on the gas.

The accident was a direct result of her speeding, but it did not shake her faith. "I would have been killed," she told all who visited her in the hospital, "but Sister Vincent was with me." We remain the best of friends, but ever since, I've worn contemporary clothes and reminded her, "I'm not wearing my power today." And she's always driven carefully.

The driving sisters do have a few accidents, but not many. Usually, the causes are the other fellow, or icy roads, or mechanical failures.

I am sure that my own success can be attributed to a little ceremony. Before I turn the key in the ignition, I say a prayer.

The prayer is for all the other drivers I'll meet along the way. I think this should be a law in every state.

A part from religious communities, the world's forgotten woman is the Mother of God.

Mary represented all that is right and just in a woman. Her humility wrapped her in a world of submission and love. She showed complete respect for authority, yet she wasn't a killjoy. Her absolute sinlessness did not prevent her from living life to the fullest degree.

A model for all times.

Quickly, now. What prominent woman of today comes close?

Is the answer the reason that so many women and their men prefer to forget Mary, or must television be the whipping boy for this, too? Poor TV!

The man was grooming a big shaggy dog. I stopped to watch and commented, "He's beautiful!"

"Thank you," said the man. "Yes, he's even better than his sire. Breed?"

He seemed to be asking a question, so I replied, "Beg pardon?"

"Your breed?"

I almost told him that I was Irish, but realized that he assumed I was another dog fancier. I was dressed in lay clothes. This was at the only dog show I've ever attended. It was quite unlike a horse show.

"I don't own any dogs," I explained.

"Well, if you're interested in sheeps, I've got some good ones ready to go at ten weeks."

"I'm sorry, but I don't have room for sheep."

He stared at me, then asked, "Are you some kind of a nut?"

I smiled, neither confirming nor denying, and walked away. Later, thanks to my friend and escort of the day, I discovered that the shaggy dog's owner was a breeder of Old English sheepdogs.

While I like dogs, I've never owned one and doubt that I ever will. My presence at the dog show that day was a result of my friend's logic. "What?" she had asked. "You've never been to one? And you talk about being involved in the real world!"

She, of course, was a dog fancier. So we went to the show, and she introduced me to many of her friends as "Sister Vincent," but I think the others assumed I was her real sister. People don't really listen to what's being said at dog shows. A great deal is said about dogs, but nobody listens.

As we drove home in the late afternoon, I observed that we had seen a couple of thousand dogs and several thousand people, but very few children. "Why do so few dog fanciers have children?" I asked.

"Plenty of them have families," my friend explained, "but on Saturdays and Sundays, the usual days for dog shows, the dogs come first. The children stay at home. I don't know why. I'm sure the youngsters would enjoy the shows. Well, what did you think of the real world?"

"It has some odd islands," I told her.

My brother Bill has three dogs. They spend their time romping with the children. I think that's the real world.

W hat do you love the mostest?" asked the child. "It's a game she plays with everybody," her mother explained, "and she means it in the material sense."

"That's easy," I told the little girl. "The thing I love the mostest is a bridge."

"Not a doll?"

"A bridge."

She didn't understand, and perhaps bridge builders will find it odd, but I love a bridge. The George Washington Bridge.

I watched it from my high-school window and from my window in St. Michaels. The bridge was my link between the old life and the new. "Crossing the bridge" to one's future is a figure of speech for most people. It was the real thing for me.

And these days, of course, I cross it to get back to the city I love the most: Manhattan. I don't know how many poems I've written in praise of both the bridge and the city. Enough to fill the pages of a fat book, certainly. And every poem is a gem—an opinion shared by my dearest friends, but not by editors.

This love for bridges runs in the family. My brother Bill loves the Golden Gate Bridge. Whenever I visit him, he drives me back and forth over that bridge precisely four times each night. This unnecessary travel has become sort of a ceremony with us. We discuss the virtues of the Golden Gate and compare them with those of the Washington. Neither bridge seems to have any sins.

And then, when I leave California, he remains convinced that his bridge is superior to mine. In a practical sense, the Golden Gate holds no special meaning for him. He has no reason for crossing it, and must go out of his way to look at it. But he loves it, and he thinks I'm silly about the George Washington.

I've found that most men are more stubborn than most women.

Among other things, involvement in the real world means diving headfirst into the very real depths of poverty, peace, and race. Those three issues are paramount, and no thinking person can avoid them. In these fast-moving times, the religious communities that fail to become involved won't have much of a future.

Some of the religious are already committed. Many others will follow. What we lack and what we need before we can become an effective force is manpower. The replacements for those leaving the Church and those going into retirement or semiretirement are not coming along in sufficient numbers. And the Church isn't about to stage a campaign to find them.

It seems strange to me that a certain segment of our society isn't responding to the Church's needs. I mean those students who are fighting for a better world that will contain peace, racial equality, and no poverty. Their aims and the Church's aims are identical, and it's about time somebody told them. Perhaps somebody has, and they weren't listening. When one is busy wrecking a campus or tearing down the Establishment, one doesn't have much time to listen.

We were told that the involved students are above average in intelligence, although I have my doubts about those who find capitalism abhorrent. Somebody must be paying their tuitions, and it's safe to bet that a few years from now—when the young ladies are wives and the young men are in business with Daddy—they'll have a change of mind.

But all the others? Just playing the laws of averages, some must be in this for the kicks, or to be known as hep, or for wanting to be where the action is. But by the same laws, some must be truly dedicated to the cause and will stay with it for the long haul.

Those are the ones who should consider the Church. If they are really interested in total commitment, if they are really sold on making this a better world, then the Church is where the action is. And will be.

So what's new in the Church?"
Renewal.
"So what's renewal?"

It's many things. The word itself appears many times in the pages of this book, and I keep telling myself that everybody understands it. But everybody doesn't. Indeed, I've met sisters who just can't grasp it, or won't grasp it, since it's difficult for them to abandon old concepts and traditions.

I regard renewal in this way: it's good news.

It means shaking the daylights out of Truth, stripping away sentiment and emotion, and thus facing the new truth of Fact.

173

And it means really living the gospel that Christ preached, but without buildup, ceremony, or ballyhoo.

And keeping both feet on a platform of love and respect and help for others.

And that "friend" is a warmer word than "benefactor."

And that "You can't beat Creation" is not a platitude.

And that my own problems is not that of being a nun, but that of being a person.

But no one will ever top Pope John's definition of renewal. He needed only two words: "Be human."

Renewal was put into motion back in 1962, and it has been moving ahead ever since. The pace is too slow for some of the religious, a little too fast for others. Disagreement is a human trait.

I don't think the general public was very aware of the new religious spirit prior to 1967, the year of our shorter hemlines. The nation's press greeted the short habit with millions of words, as if it were the entire story of renewal, whereas it was only a small, common-sense part of all that had been happening. We'd already changed the structure of internal government in many orders, traditional titles (Mother Superior, Provincial Director) were gone or going, some sisters were teaching in public schools, others were employed in industry, and still others were preparing for careers (since launched) in the battles against alcoholism and drug addiction. Even some of those who remained in the convents were active with local civic groups.

"Just what do you know about civil rights?" I asked a sister in her seventies.

"Not much, but I'm learning," she replied. "Meanwhile, I help the cause by handing out spiritual pep pills."

There's a limit to what we can accomplish under the new rules of renewal, of course. We can't work in every nook and cranny. Spreading fewer than 400,000 sisters around the country would be spreading us pretty thin. But the lid is off, so far as areas of service are concerned. There are no off-limits signs. If we can be of real help, we'll be there, but don't look for us behind the counters at Macy's.

As real people, we're becoming more involved with the real world. And wherever we come, we come as friends.

I tell you, renewal has us swinging, and I like it here.

I've never researched the belief and can't vouch for its validity, but in the good old days young ladies signed up for the convent life at the request—and often the demand—of worried parents. The reason a given set of parents was worried about daughter, of course, was that she wasn't getting any younger and probably wouldn't find a mate.

Susan B. Anthony hadn't been born, and for all I know she wasn't even a glint in her father's eyes. So there weren't many careers open for women, and the very best families gave their problem daughters to the Lord. It was a respectable thing to do, and much better than allowing their problems to hang around the house.

Over the past decade or so, many Gothic novels have started off with such a plot. And many of today's mothers have been reading those novels. I'm a minor authority for that statement. How I wish I'd kept a record of the number of times per annum that mother's have approached me after luncheons and said, following opening remarks, "Sister Vincent, would you have the time to talk to my daughter Millie?

She can't make up her mind about what she wants to do in life, and Edsel and I both feel that her exceptional talents should be devoted to the Church. As I listened to you speak, I couldn't help comparing you to Millie. You have so much in common. Oh, she's younger of course. Only twenty-nine last week." Or words to that effect.

I hope I've been doing the right thing, but I manage to avoid meeting all the Millies.

These days aren't the good old days. The parents may be fully committed to the idea of having a nun in the family, and they may be willing to build a cathedral to achieve that goal, but their hopes and their bankroll aren't enough. Millie must sell herself on the idea and then take her chances. The Lord knows we need her, but only if she feels fully committed and can make the grade. There's so much work to be done, and so little time to accomplish it.

How I'd love to reply, "Better she should stay around the apartment in Brooklyn and help her mother, which is also respectable."

Maybe I will next time.

My reputation as a nun is threatened every so often by the poor memories of old friends and associates, the ones I knew in all my prenovitiate years.

The risk is always there whenever I'm fulfilling a speaking engagement. Somebody recognizes me, stops listening, and starts remembering. Then, as soon as I sit down, he rushes to me, pumps my hand, and unleashes a barrage of words: "When I recognized you, I nearly fell off my chair! Remember me?

We were kids together on the West Side. I'm Charlie Murphy!"

"Really?" is my usual answer. I'm not too good at remembering faces. I knew many little boys on the West Side, but none was bald. "You haven't changed, Charlie."

"You have, but as soon as you started talking, I knew who you were. Say, we sure had great times when we were kids. Remember the time you set fire to the oil cans behind the garbage on 87th, and you were afraid I'd squeal to the police?"

It never happened, but now the damage is done. Twenty or thirty strangers are within hearing range, and I know from the looks on their faces that they can't wait to spread the news: "Imagine! Now she's a nun, but once she was an arsonist and had to do time!"

Denying the false accusation wouldn't help. Charlie would insist that redheads and fires are synonymous. For the next week, I'll rack my brain trying to come up with the name of the little girl who did start the fire and end up doubting my own innocence.

Sometimes I recognize the approaching old acquaintance. Following a luncheon on Long Island a few years ago, I knew that the lady behind the broad smile and under the big green hat had to be my first boss at the airline. I think it was the same hat, the one she always wore to the office, almost three decades ago.

"When I recognized you, I almost fainted!" was her greeting. I didn't consider that much of a compliment, but she meant well.

"Remember the time we sent you to Chicago," she continued, "and you left all those important papers in the taxi, and we never found them? I came close to firing you, but a certain vice-president objected. Remember him? Oh, yes, you do! We all knew you were dating him on the quiet. He never could resist a redhead. By the way, he was transferred to Los Angeles after his divorce. I don't remember whether you were subpoenaed. Is that why you entered the convent, or shouldn't I ask?"

Her memory was fair. I did lose some unimportant papers in Chicago, but they were soon recovered. I did do some special work for a certain vice-president, and several times I put in overtime, and a couple of times we went out to dinner and then returned to his office. But we never dated and never held hands, and I didn't know he liked redheads. I regarded him as a bore.

However, that Long Island ladies' organization has never asked me to speak again, and I can understand why. Who wants to listen to a husband stealer?

It is pleasant to meet old friends from the long ago, but I do wish we could expose their memories in private. Even the valid memories can be embarrassing when exposed in public. Witness this recent statement from my now elderly math teacher at junior high: "I will never forget your face, because you rank second or third on my lifetime list of extremely difficult students! You couldn't grasp anything then, and now I can't grasp how you have the talent to save souls. Tell me, did the Church study your scholastic record before accepting you? I do hope you are not in charge of funds."

She released those words of enthusiasm before a PTA dinner, and it almost wrecked my evening. I can't recall a more difficult audience, and I cut my last-on-the-menu speech to about fifteen minutes.

Still, my old teacher was among the first to congratulate me. "I'm glad I came," she assured me. "That was a very nice speech."

"You weren't too disappointed?"

"I wasn't a bit disappointed! I even learned a few things that have opened up new avenues of thought. I congratulate you! Tell me, Sister Vincent, who wrote the speech for you?"

Dear old friends and old acquaintances, wherever you are, it's so nice seeing you again, but let's discuss long ago over cups of tea.

King Melchior of Arabie, King Baltassar of Saba, and King Gaspar of Thaars are rarely mentioned anymore, but they are worth remembering in these troubled times. For those not familiar with the names, they were the Three Wise Men.

The oldest was Melchior. He was a white man and he wore a long white beard. Baltassar was middle-aged, black, and he wore a bushy black beard. Gaspar was too young to grow a beard. Since his kingdom was in the East, it's assumed he was a yellow man.

These three knelt before the Christ Child, just born of a Jewish mother.

Once upon a time, so long ago that there was no need for such terms as racism and discrimination, three very wise kings set off on a journey to find . . .

Sister, why did you become a nun?" may be the most frequently asked question in history. It is asked by men,

179

women, and children from all walks of life. Friends ask it, and strangers also feel they have a right to know. And a sister doesn't have to step outside the convent walls to hear it. One sister asks it of another.

We all wish there were one stock, acceptable answer, but there isn't. It would save a great deal of time. An inner spiritual feeling would be a basic for such an answer, but from that point on, individual reasonings would differ. To each her own.

In my case, I knew when the time for a final decision had arrived. I had three choices: a business career, marriage, and the convent. Business and marriage could have been combined, of course, to the glory of neither.

Maybe I was in the wrong business. Perhaps I hadn't met the right man. I'll never know, I don't daydream about what might have been, and I have no regrets. The convent began as a rational choice and became the right one. I consider myself to be a lucky and happy woman.

This is the life for me!

And now I am no longer Sister Vincent dePaul Quin.

In the true spirit of renewal, I have returned to my baptismal name.

Today and for the rest of my days, I am Sister Eleanor Quin, a part of this world.

❋ ❋ ❋ ❋ ❋ ❋ ❋ ❋ ❋ ❋ ❋ ❋ ❋

A Confession

This autobiography was not my idea. It was conceived and suggested by an editor who had heard me speak at a luncheon for book publishers. I was flattered, but not convinced. Then he sent me a contract.

The author's profits (if any) from this book will not be mine. They will go to my Community for the education of sisters.

Frankly, I preferred the first draft to this finished version, but it was not considered to be an autobiography. "What you have here," my editor told me, "is a love note to the individuals and groups who helped you and St. Joseph's raise that five million plus."

While their names do not appear on these pages, I wish to acknowledge the hundreds of individuals and scores of groups who made this book possible. God bless them, and all the sisters, and all the children, and all those who buy this book, and all those who don't.

Sister Eleanor Quin
St. Joseph's Home